BOOBY TRAPPED

MEN BEWARE!

THE DIRTY SEVEN SISTERS

A DATING GUIDE
FOR THE 21ST CENTURY

JUNE MARSHALL
Author of *The Dirty Seven: Ladies Beware!*

Booby Trapped: Men Beware! the Dirty Seven Sisters

Newmedia Publishing
31 Franklin Turnpike
Waldwick, NJ 07463
SAN: 253-293X

ISBN: 1-893798-28-3

Library of Congress Cataloging-in-Publication Data

Marshall, June, 1947-
   Booby Trapped: Men Beware! the Dirty Seven Sisters. A dating guide for the 21st century / by June Marshall.-- 1st ed.
      p. cm.
   ISBN 1-893798-28-3 (alk. paper) -- ISBN 1-893798-29-1 (CD-ROM)
   1. Mate selection. 2. Man-woman relationships. 3. Marriage--Psychological aspects. 4. Love. I. Title.
   HQ801.M37187 2003
   646.7'7--dc21

                                    2003010295

FOREWORD

As men, my friends and I have often been mystified by outwardly attractive women who turn into a relationship nightmare after a few dates or after the marriage vows have been exchanged. I only wish we had a guide like this to help us avoid heartache, money, and time lost. Beauty and sex notwithstanding, these women are traps: They are incapable of giving your needs fair play. This is why they are called the Dirty Seven Sisters. You will recognize some or all of them, as you read this funny and witty treatment, including documented stories of female celebrities we seem to be so entranced by today.

All of us are driven by our genes to mate, an outmoded "matter over mind" state of affairs in the 21st century. "Mind over matter" rules science, technology, and more and more of all other human endeavors today. We are now able to directly manipulate genes, the blueprints of life. With this awesome power comes responsibility: To apply our minds to find the right mates. If we don't, we will let our genes and other minds (even computers, eventually) rule over us, as we fight or abandon our mates instead of building a happy and prosperous life for ourselves and our families.

You will laugh your way through to newfound wisdom as you read this book. My wish is that you enjoy and use it to the fullest.

Steven Kingsley
Editor

TABLE OF CONTENTS

INTRODUCTION

Avoiding the Booby Traps

This book is a man's guide to choosing a date, girlfriend, wife, or lover. Its purpose is to eliminate heartache and expense for those who heed its lessons. The dating jungle is booby-trapped with dangers you may not recognize. It is not all fun and thrills when you get hooked by one of the Dirty Seven Sisters. They may be all right for one or two dates but try spending a lifetime with them and you will know the true meaning of the word "misery." TV shows like *The Bachelor, The Bachelorette, Change of Heart, The Dating Game, Who Wants to Marry a Millionaire?, Joe Millionaire, Married by America, Mr. Personality,* and *Blind Date* present a kindergartner's eye-view of dating. A man spends a few minutes with an attractive girl, surrounded by cameras, and they are now ready to get married and have children together. What if one of these beauties is a Dirty Seven Sister? We do not see that part, because it is always off camera.

Along for the Ride

Nature has played an interesting trick on you, the human male. Your brain is often just along for the ride when it comes to choosing a mate. Your penis is doing the driving and the brain is the passenger. As Robin Williams said, commenting on the Clinton/Lewinsky affair, "God gave men both a penis and a brain, but unfortunately not enough blood supply to run both at the same time." This book is designed to help you keep your mind in the driver's seat when it comes to picking women. It will give you the tools to be able to recognize and avoid the noxious and obnoxious females who are like Angel of Death mushrooms, beautiful yet deadly. Lesson #1: Beautiful does not necessarily mean good.

Sex and Survival

Your mating instincts propel you to couple with someone who is sexually attractive to you. All of nature is the same when it comes to mating. The continuation of our species depends on this attraction. Testosterone drives your body so you can reproduce yourself, as most animals do on this planet, through fertilizing a female. Male-female relationship problems would not exist if we all reproduced like amoebas, by cell division. But even animals on the more complex end of the evolutionary scale do not deal with the personality or character of their mates to the extent that we do. Horses, dogs and cats do not have mates that make their lives emotionally, psychologically, financially and physically miserable the way the Dirty Seven Sisters can make yours.

Character and Personality?

Character and personality do not figure into the mix when the silverback gorilla impregnates the females in his group, or when cur-dogs unselfconsciously mate in the street. Personality plays no role in the mating of huge flocks of look-alike penguins in the Antarctic. They are concerned about surviving the rigors of the environment. But in your case the rigors of the environment are not the issue. You are not clinging to an icy precipice, as stormy waves threaten to fling you into the Antarctic Sea. Yet the hardship of living

with one of the Dirty Seven Sisters is just as nerve-
racking. The physical threats are merely transposed to
an apartment or a house in a city or town where there is no
peace of mind, emotional safety, or happiness for you as
long as you are with her.

Who Are They?

The Dirty Seven Sisters are females who do not make good
mates, partners, wives, girlfriends, or even lovers. They
have personality and character flaws that override any other
aspect, including their good looks. You might be lured by
their looks or by the sex they offer. You have your natural
needs and these drive you toward her. However, over time
you will begin to think that the penguin's life on the
precarious iceberg is a piece of cake compared to yours. As
far as we know, a penguin's mate's behavior and attitudes
do not destroy his happiness on this earth. At least he does
not show it on his mask-like face.

Ineffective Solutions

From a primal viewpoint, you are driven by natural instincts
to reproduce and are a puppet to your genes, which run the
show and pull the strings. As a human being, you have other
needs too, such as emotional closeness and companionship.
The problem is, the way many men go about fulfilling these
needs is ineffective in the long run. When it comes to
females, the fantasy world takes over and the reality of the
woman in front of you seems irrelevant. Later you have to
deal with your poor choices: Predatory females who want to
live off of your earnings (The Material Girls); clingy, needy
basket cases who follow you around like puppy dogs
(Needee Nellies), shrewish-know-it-alls (The Moms), non-

stop talkers (Psycho Babblers), flirts who cannot settle on one man (Shopaholicas), and other examples of the Dirty Seven Sisters.

Genes in Jeans

Here is an example of the sway of fantasy over reality when it comes to female selection. You are in a nightclub full of writhing, sensual bodies throbbing to the pulse of the music. The genes in your jeans are revving up their reproductive engines. The character of the sexy female swaying her hips in front of you and bouncing her breasts is the last thing on your mind. Actually, not much is on your mind, except dreams of being with her and getting physically closer. You have had a couple of drinks, maybe some drugs. She is smiling at you and taking you in with her eyes. She wants you. You can see she is willing. The genes in your jeans take over. You leave with her and make passionate love in your car.

Years Later. . . .

You have done the right thing. You married her because she was pregnant with your baby. Your personal dreams are pushed to the back burner. You are stuck in a job you hate only because it is a steady income that provides for her and the kids. But she is impossible to live with. She is a PMS Queen. Her mood swings are unpredictable and she is constantly resentful because you cannot read her mind. You are supposed to anticipate her every need. Unfortunately, you never get it right. You are miserable and feel trapped. The punishment is way out of proportion to the crime.

Stuck

You could leave, but if you did, you'd miss your children and the alimony payments could still keep you handcuffed to your job. Besides, if you find someone else who captures your interest, she might be another type of the Dirty Seven Sisters. Thus it is important for you to use your brain to override the strange trick Nature has played on the human race. Like the baboon that is attracted to the female with the brightest red nether regions, your genes impel you to be attracted to appearances as an indication of health and suitability as a mate. Your sexuality is physically on the level of the animals, but your brain has evolved many notches beyond that level.

Getting It

It is time to move beyond our ape ancestors and employ selectivity based on something more than the sex drive. If you need to get laid on a regular basis it does not mean you have to sacrifice your life to this cause. You can choose a non-Dirty Seven Sister and still have everything else you want in your life. You can be with a great mate and also have the other things that make up a happy life:

- Interesting work and recreation
- A fulfilling emotional and sex life
- A loving and supportive partner
- Self-respect and the respect of others
- Other forms of wealth and health

Haphazard Choices

But if you get booby trapped by a Dirty Seven Sister, you will not experience much of the above, except possibly

financial wealth because you will have become a workaholic in your efforts to stay away from home. Often the
Dirty Seven Sisters take you for all you are worth too,
however, so do not count on retaining wealth either. I have
seen men who work long hours and then take their work
home at night too as a way of avoiding their partners.
Accomplishing one task after another in an endless
workload drowns out the sadness or boredom they feel
towards their home life. The workplace, especially after
hours, offers them peace and they feel they are at least in
control of something in their lives. They also see some
results for their efforts, which they do not with their Dirty
Seven Sister wives.

Family Man
Many men want to get married to someone they love and
create a happy family with her. If this is one of your main
goals in life, here is your guide to eliminating the ladies who
lure you in but later backslide when they are sure they have
snared you. The Dirty Seven Sisters do not get better with
time. If anything, they become more difficult as time passes
and their poor behavior increases to critical mass. Therefore
it is extremely important to sort through the women you are
considering. Then you will not wonder, as your PMS Queen
wife snarls and throws a cup at your head, "Where did I go
wrong? She was so beautiful and nice, before I married
her?" It is unfortunate, but some men put more thought into
buying a car than into the kind of woman they marry. So if
you do not want to be stuck with a lemon, check things out
before you buy.

Planless

Maybe you are a man who has not exactly figured out what you want to do in life. You have no plans, except to keep your head above water day by day and to have some fun at night until you decide what you want to do. Start planning, even if it is against your nature. "Too many children are the result of a bottle of whiskey on a Saturday night," (John Lennon) and you might inadvertently end up with one of them. If you are drifting around in relationships, you too can get derailed by one of these ladies. You must put thought into your love relationships or you will be thrown out into the workforce, willy-nilly, to support a family you carelessly created after a party one night.

Man Books

It is rare to see men browsing in the self-help/relationship sections of bookstore. "Men are not like that," booksellers say. "They are not going to read a book about women to avoid if they want a happy relationship. Who thinks about a chick's character issues when the testosterone is flowing freely?" Look at all the unclothed female flesh on display. What sells magazines and books? Sex! Who cares what happens after that? Boobs, butts, and other body parts on display everywhere further impel the mating instinct fueled by your genes and fantasy.

Men's Mags

As an experiment, go to a newsstand and read the topics displayed in men's magazines. You will notice that few authors deal with the subject of selecting the right mate. You might find some that focus on how to pick up, talk with, and impress a lady so she will go out with you or sleep with you.

You will find articles on keeping your love fresh, how to dress to attract, and how to behave like you know your way around a wine list and a bedroom. But you will not see much written on determining the quality of the woman for whom you are going through all that effort. You will not have much help in dealing with what happens after the first few dates. The articles are all based on the beginnings of things, not the endings. Messy endings especially are not sexy, so they don't sell.

Sex Sells
Our DNA ensures the precept that sex sells! Porn stars who were once grinding it out on cheap motel sets are now multimillionaires because of their Fee-paying Members Only websites on the Internet. One porn queen makes over a half a million dollars a month. She is in the Guinness Book of World Records for being the most downloaded woman in the world, having totaled over a billion individual viewings by paying customers. The men who download her seek the fantasy and are willing to pay for it. The problem with the Dirty Seven Sisters is that men do not realize that their fantasy is not the reality, until it is too late. By then they are paying far more for it than a year's membership to a porn site.

Stay Away!
Maybe you are the kind of man who approaches the subject of a woman's behavior like this: "I'll date her for a while and if she's too much of a pain, I'll dump her." This is fine if the dumping is done early enough. But some of the Sisters only reveal their true natures after you have married them. Then the dumping can be expensive, hurtful, and time-

consuming. You might be stuck with them in one form or another for as long as you live. Alimony is expensive and some of these Sisters' (The Material Girls) plans include milking you to the max.

Booby Trap Prevention

We all know that prevention is much less expensive than fixing a problem once it has occurred. It is cheaper to eat healthy foods than to have a triple bypass and a restricted life. The purpose of this book is preventive: To warn you up-front to stay away from these women. Bypass your DNA, which doesn't know that the gorgeous creature you want to attract is really a Needee Nellie (smothering and insecure). At first you do not see this as you cuddle with her on the couch. Her hair is soft and glistening. She looks so kissable, and she is smiling into your face. All you can think of is feeling her soft skin close to your body.

The Moment of Truth

Soon, way too soon (at her suggestion), you move in together. Now she starts showing her Needee Nellie selfhood in all its adhesive glory: She calls you every 15 minutes at work to make sure that you love her. She wants to go everywhere with you, including outings with your friends. She makes your life her life and waits by the window until you come home. How could you ever have thought that this dependent, smothering, black hole of need was sexy and appealing? It's a little late now. You are stuck with the consequences of your mindless selection process. You can move out, but that may not be the end. She might continue to call you, even stalk you, because she needs you so badly. Then you realize: You've been booby trapped by one of the Dirty Seven Sisters!

We're No Angels

It is time for many of us women to be honest with ourselves. Some of us have gotten away with blaming men for too many of our relationship difficulties. Our own behavior may be at fault. One of the reasons our behavior is not called into question may be that the majority of "how to" relationship books and articles are written by women. The topics they choose are what publishers and marketers think will sell to women: How to attract, understand, and keep a man. They do not address a woman's basic character as a possible relationship killer or keeper. They do not go into what makes a woman worthy of attracting and keeping a relationship with a good mate.

Character Magazine

Like men's magazines, women's periodicals focus on physical appearance with a tilt towards fashion and surface. A glossy magazine called *Character,* featuring inwardly beautiful people, would not be a big seller. It would be like the nightly news reporting on all the people not murdered, raped, or swindled. Good news does not sell papers or magazines. How many people would want to watch the Jerry Springer show if it were about people solving their problems reasonably, helping each other, and being thoughtful? *Confidential* magazine, which had record sales when it reported dirt on celebrities, went out of business when it began to publish only positive stories about these people. It's no fun to read about people behaving well and showing good character.

Hollywood Fantasies

Being easy to live with is not an exciting subject that stimulates strong emotions of desire, envy, yearning, and sexuality. The soap operas would quickly fizzle without scandalous high jinx and betrayals. A movie about a happy couple living peacefully together would be a yawn! Hollywood understands this and does not produce any. But a movie about how a gorgeous girl sets about to sabotage her best friend's wedding and steal away with the groom, grosses millions of dollars. This beauty is a weasel. But she is a stylish weasel who goes through the scenes with a carefree smile, flipping her curls over her twinkling eyes. She is so sexy and yet so girl-next-door! Only a nerd would question, "What kind of a back-stabber would do such an underhanded thing to a friend?"

Unhappily Ever After

Movies obviously cater to the fantasy world of appearances and escape. Their creators know that moviegoers are not really interested in delving into issues of character and disposition, especially as related to beautiful women. To be beautiful is to be good, or, conversely, to be a beautiful femme fatale is evil, in an exciting way (Lena Olin in *Romeo is Bleeding*). You will not see too many Dirty Seven Sisters in the movies. No one wants to see a film about what it is like to live with a behaviorally deficient, constant pain-in-the-neck. The public is unwilling to pay money to see such discomfort. It seems too much like real life. Why pay for what they might have at home? It only has entertainment value as comedy. But the actuality is no laughing matter.

The Dirty Seven: Ladies Beware!

In my first book, *The Dirty Seven: Ladies Beware!*, I describe the types of dead-end men women must avoid if they are looking for happiness with a mate. If a lady stays with one of them, she is destined to giving far more than she receives from a man who does not pull his weight in the relationship. His "me-ism," or lack of empathy, results in behaviors that wear the woman down with aggravation, annoyance, exasperation, frustration, and stress. Therefore, the only solution is to pass on them completely, or get out if already involved. Like the Dirty Seven Sisters, these men only get worse over time.

Underlying Problems

The Dirty Seven Sisters have different problems than their male counterparts. With the men, me-ism is the common thread that unites each of the Dirty Seven characters. With the Dirty Seven Sisters, it is not as clear-cut. Some of them manifest a certain inner emptiness, which cancels them out as good mates (Needee Nellie, The Material Girl, and The Wedding Belle). Some have control issues (The Mom, The PMS Queen). One has reliability, consistency, and sincerity problems (Shopaholica). One humorlessly dissects even the smallest things in the relationship until it dies or stalks you emotionally until you rue the day you ever met (The Psycho Babbler).

Bait and Switch

One characteristic that many of the Seven Sisters have in common is the bait and switch tactic. They act and look one way before you move in together or get married. After they have bagged their mates, they do not make the effort to be nice or considerate anymore. They let themselves go physically, emotionally, or intellectually. Exceptions exist such as the Pretty Pennies, who spend their lives self-grooming and make no pretense of having any depth even at the beginning. Psycho Babblers also show their hand by examining the relationship intensely from the outset, often rushing the inspection before you even know it is a relationship. Needee Nellies will also give you some warning about themselves up front, when your Caller ID registers how often they call after only a few dates.

Move on
Pass on them, unless you want to hold their hands through therapy, which may take years, with no guarantee of success. Personality problems are very difficult to cure. You may wind up going to therapy yourself, thinking it is your problem. It will become your problem if you stay with them. If you have masochistic tendencies these women are right for you. But if you are not fascinated with problem behavior, or are more comfortable with happiness than misery, stop! You will not find peace and joy with any one of these personality types. If you are looking for a girlfriend or a wife who adds to your life instead of sapping energy from it, recognize these Dirty Seven Sisters and move on.

Idealizing Women
It is important for you to get this message one more time. If a woman is beautiful, it does not necessarily mean she is a good mate. The beauty and fashion industry, which financially support most women's magazines, want women to focus on looking beautiful so they will continually buy new products. Men's girlie magazines show airbrushed,

enhanced beauties that inspire fairy-tale breaks from reality. It is easy to idealize a beautiful woman because her perfect face and flawless body excite the same center in the brain (the parietal lobe) that is responsible for the ecstasy of religious experience. What a harsh trick though, when you discover that sweet-faced, ethereal blonde is one of the Dirty Seven Sisters. She is The Mom (bossy, knows everything better than you do) and those soft curves do not block out the nagging.

Frumpy Demons

If you are a man who has been burned by one of the dangerous beauties and think that you will go for a plainer package next time, beware as well. Dirty Seven Sisterhood is no respecter of appearances. Just as fabulous can sometimes be evil, so can just plain frumpy. Men are less inclined to be fooled by frowsy or poorly groomed women than by hotties. This is because they are not attracted to them enough to take the next step and care about their character. Often they will stereotype them as kindly and harmless because they have opted out of the appearance shark pool and try to slip by unnoticed. Warning: Appearance has nothing to do with Dirty Seven Sisterhood. It is all about what is going on inside the woman. That is what you will have to live with.

An Inside Job

Finding the right mate is an inside job. This means it is about finding out what is going on inside the woman you are with. Does she show her beautiful soul and spirit? Does she have a sense of humor that helps her and you through the rough patches of life? Does she talk to you with respect for your personhood? It is also an outside job in the sense that it is about how she behaves. Someone can talk like she has a beautiful soul and yet act like a screaming banshee when you share living quarters with her on a daily basis. She can be unreliable except for being reliably late, sloppy, and draining.

Ain't Misbehavin'

Many women talk a good game. They can pretend to be low-maintenance flower children when they are really drama queen fairy princesses who have hissy fits if they aren't the stars of every show. They can pretend to be acting any number of fairy tale roles over candle-lit dinners and romantic music, while they lay their trap for you. In time their behavior shows them to be the warty troll you only wish lived under the bridge and not with you!

A Man's Own Words

Bob, a seasoned dater, explained it to me this way, "What's really strange is how the DNA and its survival mechanisms start to play tricks on you. Over the weekend I found myself having totally retarded conversations with pretty girls, and actually being interested in whatever dumb bullshit we were talking about. I would smile, and keep talking when ordinarily I would have probably politely excused myself and headed for the exit.

"See, that's one of the weird things about men that most women aren't aware of. A lot of women think that men will tell you almost anything that you want to hear, and pretend they're interested in what you have to say, just to get some sex. But the reality is that the men, for the most part, aren't even aware of it when they're doing it. It's not really a conscious decision to be full of shit for the most part (although many men will lie and tell you that it is).

"It's really sorta like you're in some testosterone induced hypnotic trance, like cock auto pilot or cruise control. After you blast off, the trance is gone, and you're just sitting there confused. I can't tell you how many times I've had sex with a chick, and after it was over I was actually confused. I was sitting there thinking:

"Here I am naked, lying in bed with someone I have absolutely nothing in common with, after wasting an entire evening talking to her about retarded bullshit just so I could get some sex, and I wasn't even aware of what I was doing until now.

"Then after the girl senses this, they start to harp on you: Well, I guess you got what you wanted, and now you just want to leave. . . Then the real, conscious lies start. The lies that you tell to try to smooth the situation over so that you can make as guilt free an exit as possible. The lies about work to do in the morning, the lies about having had a great time. . .The most evil lie of all: I'll call you.

"Now, don't get me wrong, I'm not saying that this happens with all sexual interactions between men and women, but for me at least, these kind are surely the most confusing. These are the ones that are purely animal, and totally DNA driven. They CERTAINLY aren't the best ones.

"When men and women click, it is truly a fantastic, amazing

thing. I love very few things in life more than hanging out with a hot chick with a great sense of humor. Having a great date, with a really fun, intelligent girl is one of the most magical things in all of life for me, but. . . if there's no smart, hot chicks around, I will trick myself into having a cheap evening with a hot dumb-dumb."

A Final Word about Alimony
That cheap evening with a hot dumb-dumb might lead to your entrapment through her pregnancy and one day to a divorce, in which she smartly takes half your earnings. Look at the large alimony settlements some ex-wives are getting. The largest was in 1998: $44 million to a housewife who felt she was entitled to half her husband's earnings even though she did nothing outside of the home to build that fortune. She, like many others, enjoyed the fine lifestyle supported by her high-achieving husband, including household help, caterers, nannies, club member-ships, and a social whirl of vacations and parties. The legal system supports and thrives on this kind of parasitism. Awareness is the only thing that can save you from being booby trapped!

THE DIRTY SEVEN SISTERS:
WHO THEY ARE

The Dirty Seven Sisters are women who have earned their membership in this sisterhood by not being good mates, partners, wives, girlfriends, or even lovers. They are the:

- **PMS Queen:** Perpetually Menstrual Shrew, mood-swinging drama-queen diva.
- **Needee Nellie:** Clingy, emotional black hole of endless need.
- **The Material Girl:** All about money, consumer goods, and appearances.
- **Shopaholica:** Looking for someone better but keeping you around until it happens.
- **Wedding Belle:** A storybook wedding is her life. She is already naming the kids on the first date.
- **The Mom:** She knows best. You are just one of the kiddies.
- **Psycho Babbler:** Nutty non-stop talker who analyzes the relationship to death.

Merely Dirty

Though the Dirty Seven Sisters are a pain and make you wonder, "What was I thinking?," they are not filthy. I assume you have the common sense to stay away from the Filthy Seven Sisters, who are absolute and unqualified life-wreckers. They are the alcoholics and hard drug addicts whose first love is their substance of choice. They are also the criminal types who abuse children and physically attack men, unprovoked. They are the ones who carry venereal diseases and do not tell you because they hate all men and think you deserve whatever you get. Or, they are the cold-hearted killers after the proceeds of your life insurance. Maybe they are the ladies who are hookers on the side but tell you they earn their money in a straight job. No, this book does not address these types of women. The Dirty Seven Sisters are a higher life form than the Filthy Seven, but they will make you miserable, nevertheless.

Irritating but Tolerable
Some women exhibit behaviors that border on the Dirty Seven Sisters but do not qualify as life wrecking or happiness destroying. These are not fundamental character or personality flaws but can create a bad aftertaste because they are aggravating. For example, the diet-obsessed female who thinks everyone is as interested in her latest weight-loss plan as she is. She is boring and annoying but is not a blood-sucking drain on your life's energy. The triviality of her preoccupation with her weight and the latest diet shows her to be a shallow fad-follower with not much more on her mind that her bodyweight.

I'm on a Diet!
A whole group of behaviors crop up around being on a diet that can be irritating. The first is constantly talking about how many calories she consumed and enumerating every cookie or piece of candy she ate that day, especially when she is out dining with you. Her conversation goes something like this: "Oh my God! I ate three chocolate chip cookies today and six potato chips! Oh God! I also had a quarter of a

candy bar and a teaspoonful of ice cream! I had five cashews, four jelly beans (two lemon/lime flavored and two cherry) and drank a quarter of a bottle of orange soda. And I couldn't help myself, I also had a bite of a donut someone brought in at work today! I had three pieces of lettuce for lunch with no dressing and some sugarless gum. I also cheated and put some yolks into my eggwhite omelet for breakfast. I drank a diet shake for lunch and had six French fries without the ketchup and I went 159 calories over my diet! Tomorrow I will have to make up for it by starving myself all day long. Oh, I forgot to mention the three M&Ms I ate on my way to work!"

Missing the Point

One of the problems with this sort of behavior is that it counteracts the purpose of the diet, which is to make her more attractive. It's like the woman who wears hair curlers poking out of a ratty scarf in public so she will look good later in the day. Why bother? In this case, the unattractiveness of babbling on about every morsel of food she consumes makes her striving for physical perfection ludicrous. Not only is it tiresome, but it shows the emptiness of her life. If she is that consumed by every detail of what crosses her lips and makes it into her stomach, not much else is going on in her world. That she thinks you could be interested in such blather shows she is clueless about what makes up a real conversation.

I'm not Eating Anything

Another vexatious dieting behavior pattern occurs when you are out to eat and it is time to order from the menu. She looks over the entire bill of fare and declares she is on a diet. She will only order salad, with no dressing. Then, when your meal comes she eyes it with longing and hunger. She reaches across to your plate and starts picking away at your food, sometimes eating more than half of your dinner because she is starving! You say to her, "Why don't we order something for you?" She replies, "Oh, no! I'm on a diet and I can't break it!"

However, as irritating and senseless as this behavior is, it is nothing compared to the attitudes and actions in the chapters that follow.

THE PMS QUEEN

MOOD SWINGER

On the Rag

The PMS Queen is one of the most difficult of the Dirty Seven Sisters because of her behavior patterns (or lack of patterns). The acronym PMS normally stands for Premenstrual Syndrome. In her case, it stands for Perpetual Menstrual Shrew, occurring in three phases: Pre Menstrual, Positively Menstrual, and Post Menstrual. You do not know exactly which P-phase she is in because her mood swings defy prediction, but she is always in one of them. You learn that her life and yours is divided into three segments:

- **Pre Menstrual:** She is just about to have her period. Watch what you say to avoid unwanted explosions!
- **Positively Menstrual:** She is actually having her period. Watch that expression on your face. She won't like it, whether you are smiling (how can you be happy when she is so miserable?), or frowning (even if you try you can never know what she is going through), or just being neutral (how can you be neutral when she is suffering so much?).
- **Post Menstrual:** She is just getting over her period. Be careful, you are getting on her last nerve, which is raggedly on the breaking point. Even sneezing might set her off ("Cover your mouth! Do you have to sneeze so loud?")

Excuses, Excuses

Being Pre, Positively, and Post Menstrual is the excuse for why you never know what kind of response you will get from her. In reality, she may not really have PMS, which is a legitimate medical syndrome. She just acts as if she did. You walk through the door, yawning after a long day of work and commuting. She looks at you and sneers. "You yawned! What kind of a hello is that? You can have dinner on your own tonight if that's what you think of me! Don't you know I'm just about to get my period and everything is going wrong in my life? All you can do is yawn!"

You are tired and did not get much sleep last night because she wanted to stay up discussing why she is so unhappy with you. You thought you could come home to relax after your active day. But going home to relax will not be possible if you live with a PMS Queen. You are tiptoeing through a booby-trapped minefield. With each step, something might explode in your face and usually does.

The Moody Blues

When you met her she was interesting, energetic, and fun. Somehow she is not so cute anymore. Her tearful and angry outbursts distort her features. Her nose is bloated and red from crying. You walk on eggshells around her. Who knows what will set her off next or what variation of temper tantrum she will act out? Or maybe you stay at work longer or hang out with your friends more just to avoid the emotional turmoil of being around her. You think, "Maybe all women act this way." She is giving you the moody blues. You are blue because she is moody. You cannot live with someone who is continuously angry and not be affected.

Happy men turn bitter and cynical from cohabiting with their PMS Queens over the years unless they tune them out.

The Party's Over
One of the problems is that the PMS Queen's mood swings do not swing up to any of the positive emotions. They oscillate only in the negative ranges (except in front of others, when she makes the effort to appear nice). They swing between negative and more negative: From anger to fear, to suspicion, to crankiness, to jealousy, to hopelessness. You think back to when you met her. Did she give you any clues she was like this? She was on her best party and date behavior then. Now that she has trapped you, she doesn't need to pretend or make an attempt at being friendly, open, and warm to you at least. She lets her true disposition show. She might not even bother to fix herself up any more. You look across the room to see her huddled in her grungy bathrobe, unwashed hair clinging to her scalp, in all her PMS Royalty: complaining, angry, sullen, and impossible to make happy.

A NO-WINNER

Mission Impossible
If your mission in life is to prove that you can make the PMS Queen happy, give it up now. She will never be happy, is incapable of happiness, and certainly cannot find it through the efforts of someone outside herself. She is the victim of her own self-pity. She feels she has no control over her emotions. She is being hormonal and that excuses everything. She is just a victim of the cycles of the

moon! She does not even try to gain mastery over her reactivity, she is just a puppet whose strings are controlled by the chemical forces circulating through her bloodstream. She thwarts your every effort to make her happy, as if to prove how right she is: You are a loser. If you bring her flowers they are not the kind she likes. If they are the kind she likes, you didn't bring enough, or you brought too many. Whatever you try, you lose.

Constant Outrage
The PMS Queen is called "Queen" because she believes the world is there to make her happy. But the world and you are failing miserably. She wakes up in the morning and is immediately outraged at how things are not cooperating with her. She drops her toothbrush, she cannot find the shirt she wants to wear, there is no coffee, and it's raining! The world is making her angrier and angrier. You get in her way as she enters the bathroom. She launches a tirade about how inconsiderate you are. You used up the coffee last and you should have gotten more. You know how much she needs it and now she doesn't have any! Do not think you will be "getting any" either, tonight or even this week. Besides, she is just about to have her period and has cramps. She is very, very miserable and it's all your fault!

I'm Not OK, You're Not OK
The PMS Queen is an example of the age-old saying, "Misery loves company." She wants you to be as unhappy as she is. It's lonely being so depressed and angry all the time. She wants you to share her unhappiness with her, and she will do her best to make sure you do. If you try to do something to make things better, you are actually going

against her purposes. You are in a bind. If you do not act to make things better, you are a creep. If you do try to make things better she will take delight in showing you how it only makes things worse. Maybe you decide to go out to get the coffee. She is enraged, "Too little, too late, as usual," she says. "Besides, this is just another example of how inconsiderate you are! If I wait for you to return with the coffee, I'll be late to work! Anyway, you always get that cheaper brand that I hate!"

Mind Reader
One game you are sure not to win with the PMS Queen is the Mind Reader Game. She expects you to read her mind about why she is angry with you or why she is upset in general. You are supposed to be able to interpret her expressions of exasperation and irritation and pinpoint exactly what you said or did to cause them. It might take you all night to unearth the fact that she is angry with you because that morning you said, "Have a nice day," in a tone of voice she did not like. The fact that you have not read her mind about this, only compounds her annoyance as the hours pass. What an insensitive lout you are for not knowing how sarcastic you sounded when you said that to her! She has been fuming about it all day and you do not even have a clue about how unhappy you have made her!

THE PMS QUEEN MOTHER

Pity the Defenseless
If you see a future with children in it, you need to put thought into a woman's potential qualities as a mother. This

includes what kind of example she will set for the lifetime of those kids. Pity your poor offspring if they have a PMS Queen for a mother. They do not know when or where the next explosion will come and for what reason. There is no consistency to give them a sense of emotional security. Her crying jags and screaming fits keep the kids, like the man in her life, tiptoeing around the minefield, never knowing what will set her off. She will punish a child severely for not tying his shoes one day and gently tie those same shoes for him the next. She will console a child for losing a toy one day and smack her the next day for the same thing because the thought of it suddenly made her angry.

Having children is too easy and there are no tests people must pass to qualify them for parenthood. The future of the world depends on our children but who thinks of that while banging away in the backseat after a hot date? You must think of it if you do not want your life and the lives of your children to be a living hell.

PMS Queen Examples

Mourning Person

Melissa was stunningly attractive. Her originality and sense of style drew Kevin in the first day he met her. She was clever, knowledgeable, and wise about a broad range of subjects. He counted himself a lucky man that she was also interested in him. He felt a sense of connection with her on their dates. He could not imagine life without her and eventually asked her to marry him.

It was a mistake! After their wedding, even on their honeymoon, Melissa showed her true Godzilla-like nature in the morning. Kevin didn't have a clue that Melissa was the Wrath of God in the beginning of each and every day. Most of their dates had been in the evening or late afternoon. During the times they saw each other in the morning, Melissa had managed to consume her mandatory five cups of coffee. He thought it was cute that she was not a morning person, and they both laughed about it.

Now they do not laugh much about anything in each other's company. Her nasty remarks in the morning hang over his mind throughout the day. When he returns home, it seems that morning has bled into evening, because Melissa is in the same bad mood. If he had known she was a PMS Queen, he would not have combined his life with hers.

Rescue Me!
Some PMS Queens expect you to fix whatever is wrong in their lives. They grew up believing in the Knight-in-shining-armor Theory, whereby the man is supposed to rescue them and they will live happily ever after. They do not build inner resources for coping with life's problems. Instead, they wait to attract a man into their net, to do it for them. Then, when the man cannot make everything right all the time, they turn on him and hate him for letting them down. Now he is part of the problem and deserves the blame. He too is swept into the vortex of their anger and he is the one who is going to hear about it. "How wrong it is for a woman to expect the man to build the world she wants, rather than to create it herself." (Anais Nin)

This was the case of Jessica and Marcus. Jessica had spent her life dreaming about attracting a man who could take care of her. Usually she was irritable and touchy because things didn't go her way every minute. She thought it was enough for Princess Jessica to wish it and it would come true. But she had to go to work and earn a living like everyone else and this was not her dream life. She knew when she met Marcus, her life was going to change. He was going to fix everything. He was going to save her from this annoying existence. He was psychologically healthy and had the bright spirit that was missing from her dark inner world.

After the extravagant wedding and honeymoon, they settled down to life with each other. Unfortunately, she still had to wake up in the morning (what an effort!); keep things clean (that damn dirt keeps coming back in spite of wishing it away!) and earn money (it should just come to her because she wants it!). The world was not breathlessly waiting to obey her every command. She began to blame Marcus. He had really disappointed her. Life was still life -- the same as before they got married. Things still did not go her way every time. She still had to make an effort. She was still in perpetual PMS. He failed her! He failed her! She despised him and would never forgive him for dashing her lifelong hopes! Every day of their marriage she was going to remind him that he never did and never would make her happy!

Crybaby
One type of PMS Queen isn't angry. She is just sad and weepy. Mandy was a Crybaby PMS Queen. She was contented around her friends, but around her husband,

Jamie, she spent much time crying, whining, and giving him the silent treatment because he didn't understand why she was feeling that way. Her psychiatrist told her she was depressed, but Jamie didn't need to hear that diagnosis as it was obvious to him. He felt bad for her. How had she managed to be cheerful before they got married?

It was depressing going home to Mandy. Jamie felt a strange sense of guilt. What was it about him that elicited this behavior from his wife? He wasn't doing anything differently from when they were first going out. If she was really mentally ill, he believed it was possible to seek a cure, but Mandy was getting a big pay-off from her "poor-little-me" routine. She experienced a certain degree of satisfaction in being a figure of pity for her husband. She could sit and cry while he took care of the household. She just couldn't deal with any of it. When the vacuum cleaner's cord got tangled up, Jamie found her crumpled in a sobbing mass on the floor. "I'll fix it for you, honey," he said kindly. All she could do was weep.

Jamie was looking ahead to the time when they would have children. But his friend Paul was also married to a Crybaby PMS Queen. Jamie knew Paul was taking care of the children now and holding down a night job because his wife could not cope with child care duties. He was paying a baby sitter at night to take up the slack, while his wife sat and did nothing. Paul had confided to Jamie about how trapped and guilty he felt. He knew his wife was sick, but it still didn't make his life any happier or easier. Somehow he felt responsible and was doing all he could but it still was not enough.

Nice Man/Bitch Combos

Many of us have been stymied by the phenomenon of the bitchy woman mated with the super nice man. It happens so often and it defies all logic. The man has a lot going for him and she is no great shakes. And, on top of it all, she acts like a bitch most of the time. In some cases the man is like a hamster on a non-stop wheel, running in circles to find ways of pleasing his shrewish mate. Angie is a bitter, complaining, nagging, sourpuss example of this strange combo. She was married to Rich, an even-tempered, easy-going man. He did extra things to try to bring a smile of approval to her twisted little face. Angie told all her acquaintances (she didn't have any friends, because her sullen ways extended to women too) that she and Rich never argued or fought.

They never fought because Rich gave into her every whim and didn't want to make waves, which would make his gloomy life with her even more difficult. He was whipped! However, avoidance of conflict still does not make the PMS Queen happy, because nothing does. Do not think you will be the one to rescue someone like Angie from her mental funk: Staying with her will not make her happy, leaving her will not make her happy, nothing will make her happy. She is determined to prove to the world that she is right about this and all your efforts will only prove her more correct.

Tuning out, Turning off

Tim and Sandra were a bitch/nice man combination. Sandra yammered complaints non-stop whenever Tim was at hand. One day I asked him, "Tim, how do you cope with the constant ill-humor?" He pointed to his hearing aids and said, "I take them out sometimes. For other occasions, I have developed a method of tuning her out so her tantrums sound like white noise to me, equivalent to a soft jack-hammer in perpetual motion."

No one could understand why Tim put up with this. He was attractive, wealthy, and admired by men and women alike. But some men get used to misery in their lives and it becomes normal to them. It is comfortable, because it is what they know. Like the battered child, screaming for his mother as the social service agent takes him away, she is all the mother he has ever known and that is what a mother is to him. Tim began to think of his PMS Queen as the norm. He had become used to the low-level misery that was his daily habit.

Nag, Nag, Nag!
Griffith told his story this way, "I'm married to the Queen of Naggers and I don't think I can take another minute of her bickering, complaining, and harassment. From the moment I arrive, she starts her nagging and never lets up until I hit the sack.

"It has come to the point where the only communication between the two of us is when she tells me all the things I did wrong during the course of the day, week, month, or since we've been married.

"The situation has become so bad that I'm even asking my boss for overtime work. Can you imagine that? I'd rather stay at work than go home. The stress of listening to her complaints is so strong that I get headaches while driving home from work. It shouldn't be like this. I should be excited about leaving work and getting home to my wife."

PMS Queen Celebrity Examples

Bloody Queens
Tawny Kitaen, Lorena Bobbitt, and other husband batterers
have become news items of interest to the public. Phil
Hartman is no longer alive because of his PMS Queen wife
and neither is Spider Savitch the international ski star when
Claudine Longet pulled the trigger. These women are not
career criminals, who are automatically excluded from the
Dirty Seven Sisters. They just let their moods get out of
hand to the point of a lapse in their sanity. Most female
celebrities hide their evil tempers because it wouldn't be
good publicity. But when they push it to illegal proportions
the public finds out as the bruised, battered, and dead bodies
of their mates bear witness.

Queen Divas
It is difficult to get an honest look at the true nature of our
female celebrities, away from the pearly-toothed images
portrayed in the sycophantic glossies and filtered
interviews. We do not often get to see their demanding,
vain, humorless, and self-obsessed sides. But we get a
glimpse of some of their PMSisms when we hear that
Mariah Carey has a fit if she doesn't have the exact shade of
pink toilet paper in her travels. Faye Dunaway insists that
everyone in the studio cafeteria leave the room if they are
wearing red, because she cannot stand the color. Madonna,
during her MTV stay in Stockholm, insists that her suite be
repainted in a completely different color. She follows the

Liz Taylor example, who once demanded that the Dorchester Hotel in London repaint her room lilac while she was staying there.

The Celebrity PMS Queens demands' and the hissy fits they throw if they aren't satisfied are ridiculous, but woe betide anyone who gets in their way. An example is a report about Meg Ryan on the set of *Against the Ropes*. She has the perky girl-next-door image but threw a tantrum and had several members of the catering crew fired because her grapes and cheese were the wrong temperature. By definition these divas behave badly and irrationally and embarrass themselves outrageously without shame, grace, or dignity.

Naomi
Supermodel Naomi Campbell is infamous worldwide for her rudeness and temper tantrums. She was voted the Most Hated Woman in England for 2002. It seems that the beauteous Naomi falls out with many people who cross her path. Famous moments include a screaming match with Donatella Versace, who dropped her as a model when she demanded an exorbitant fee. She was eventually let go by Elite Model Management who described her as "a manipulating, scheming, rude and impossible little madam." Immortalized in the play *Fully Committed* for her moody demands, she once insisted that a New York restaurant reopen its kitchen early in the morning and make her special soup, which she afterwards did not eat. She also insisted on her social secretary bringing special light bulbs in case Ms. Campbell's beauty might be marred by glare.

An assistant, Ms. Galanis, filed a lawsuit in New York's Supreme Court against Naomi. Galanis lasted only a week working for the tempestuous Campbell. She claims that during her September stint, Campbell twice struck her in the head with a telephone while grabbing her by the neck, then never bothered to pay her. Naomi later underwent treatment for anger management and drug abuse. Nevertheless, she reportedly swallowed a fistful of tranquilizers following a fight with her onetime lover, Joaquin Cortes.

Mariah

Exhibiting levels of queenly tardiness like that of Naomi Campbell and J-Lo, Mariah showed up two hours late at the 2000 World Music Awards to collect an award for best-selling artist of the millennium alongside Michael Jackson. When she did arrive, she threw a furious fit because she thought Michael had been given more of a superstar build-up than her. She demanded the award be given to her again. Recently she kept motorists waiting in a mile-long string of traffic in London when she parked her limo illegally so she could apply her make-up. Other diva-demands included having a litter of puppies and kittens with her while on-set for her MTV appearance in London. Additionally, she asked 20 assistants to completely redecorate a shop toilet because she wanted to use it during an in-store signing. She also apparently pulled out of one television interview when she found out she would be expected to walk down some stairs. "Ms. Carey doesn't do stairs."

Whitney

Whitney Houston is known as "Queen Diva of Hotels." Hotels worldwide must cringe and shudder when they see her name on their guest list. One such example involved Whitney and her husband Bobby Brown. They were actually banned from the Hotel Bel-Air in California for causing approximately $30,000 in damage to their room during a three-hour brawl. Alleged damage included broken doors, a smashed crystal table and a trampled 27-inch TV set. Such appalling and childish behavior shows a self-indulgent and self-absorbed individual who insists on absurd and perverse demands. Additional examples are: Having an assistant go into rooms ahead of her to make sure she won't be too hot or cold when she finally steps inside, as well as having her bath checked with a thermometer before poking her delicate toe into the water. She also held up a video shoot for four hours once because she did not like the chair in her dressing room.

J-Lo
Nobody tops favorite diva, Jennifer Lopez. Her ludicrous expectations include being ushered from A to B in a black Mercedes with a male driver and her coffee stirred counter-clockwise. Other requirements include: Sheets with a certain thread count, full-length mirrors in every room; Body Shop body butter available to her at any given time of day, burning candles in her rooms, an expensive fragrance sprayed into her path as she walks, an electric fan blowing her hair just the right way, and accommodations for a posse of up to 60 people.

In December 1999 the police picked up J-Lo and P. Diddy following a shoot-out at a New York nightclub. A tantrum erupted and hysterics ensued, not because of mistreatment by police or not getting access to her lawyer or being held unfairly but because they were holding her without access to her cuticle cream. To remedy this life-threatening situation, an officer was sent on a mission to procure some cuticle cream and J-Lo was happy for the moment.

Tonya

Poor little PMS Queen Tonya Harding was arrested for ripping off a hubcap and beating her husband with it in a fit of rage. Technically, she is not one of the Dirty Seven Sisters because they do not include criminals but she is here as an example of the kind of behaviors in which a PMS Queen might typically indulge. In the past, she had ordered the clubbing and wounding of her rival skater, Nancy Kerrigan, and continues to be outraged that people bring it up. "I said I'm sorry for what I did. How many times do I have to say it?" She must not have been sorry enough about her behavior when she ploughed into her husband.

In another incident, she could not get it together to arrive on time to her eviction hearing and was thrown out of her dwelling for owing over $5,000 in rent.

Trouble, trouble, trouble follows the PMS Queens around like a shadow. Their little lives are more important than anyone else's and they keep people waiting to show where their priorities are. Their number one priority is, of course, showing the world that they are The Queens and above the considerations of common folk.

Leona

Leona Helmsley, also known as The Queen of Mean, is famous for her condescending and cutting remarks, "Only little people pay taxes," and "If I'm not happy, you won't be happy." Tales of her disciplinarian tactics with her hotel employees have become legends of cruelty and public humiliation. Her harsh personality has yielded her few friends, but she was notoriously protective of her deceased husband Harry, whom she treated with tenderness. Thus, though her public personality displays characteristics of the PMS Queen, her private personality does not. However, she does have special meals prepared for her dog "Trouble," whom she reportedly treats better than she treats humans.

Prevention: Stop, Look, Listen

Stop
Because the Dirty Seven Sisters bait and switch, it is sometimes not easy to determine if your love interest is a PMS Queen. However, she will slip up a few times during the dating period. When the relationship is new, and especially if the woman is attractive, you might make all kinds of excuses for occasional irrational squalls. You may even think this shows she has spirit and isn't bland, a positive thing. But be aware that the chemistry between you may blind you to what she is really like. If she already erupts into tantrums six months into the relationship, acts sulky, expects you to read her mind, or acts like she is royalty and her whims are more important than anyone else's, it may spell trouble. That is why it is a good idea to have a long waiting period before marriage. How else can you see how she behaves over time? Stop. Do not rush into things.

Look

Observe her actions, not just how great her butt looks in jeans. That vision of loveliness across the room sparks your desire for love, sex, fantasy, adventure, and play. What you may end up with over time is faultfinding, frostiness, and more mood swings than a playground in a psycho ward. Unless she is wearing a mood-swing timer that gives you a digital read-out of her state of mind, you will have to use simple observation and patience.

See how she handles a crisis. Does she go to pieces and carry on out of proportion to the event? Does she obsess all day long and into the next over losing an earring? Is the expression on her face becoming more and more negative now that she doesn't have to wear her dating smile? Those are some of the questions to ask yourself before you combine your life with a PMS Queen.

Listen

Even on your first date, you can discover a lot from conversation. Notice not only what she says, but also how she expresses it. Is she already whining and complaining about the restaurant, the food, and the people that surround you, what a horrible day she has had so far and how miserable life is in general? Does she offer feedback of any kind to what you say? Or is it all about her and her important Queendom? Does she know how to laugh at a joke? Usually PMS Queens take even trivial things far too seriously and have a meager sense of humor, especially about themselves. They take the simplest remarks personally. Even if you say something as harmless as, "Have a nice day," she might take it personally and respond with, "I'm tired of you men telling me what to do. I'll have any kind of damn day I want, thank you, and if I want to have a miserable day, by God, I will have a miserable day! Who the hell are you to tell me what kind of day to have? Sure, I'm PMS-ing, but how would you like it if you had to deal with getting your period every month? You wouldn't, would you? So take your 'Have a nice day' and put it where the sun doesn't shine!"

NEEDEE NELLIE

A HOLE YOU CANNOT FILL

The Abyss
Needee Nellie is the female with no inner life (and no outer life either). Her first name ends with a double "e" for doubly empty. She depends on you to provide her reason for living. She is so vacuous and insecure, she sucks the life out of you through her endless need, if you let her glom onto you. She is the woman who calls you on the phone every half-hour with, "Do you love me? Are you sure you love me? How much do you love me?" She tries to be with you at all times, even when you are out with your friends at football games, fishing trips, or poker nights. She is not interested in these activities, but she has to be around you as much as possible because she has no life of her own. She is an abyss of need and she wants you to fill her up. But no one can give her as much love as she needs, because her needs are oceanic in capacity.

The Black Hole
She sits by the window waiting for you to come home. She sits by the phone waiting for you to call. She is scared you will not call. You are the meaning of her life, because she has very few important interests of her own. Her only interest is you. This may be flattering at first, but she puts tremendous pressure on you to be her everything. She is so dense with need, she sucks the energy out of you, like the black hole in space that sucks everything into its vortex, including light. When she is with her friends, which is rare,

she bores them with endless talk about you, and stops in the middle of the monologue to call you to tell you she loves you. If you stay with her, you will feel your light being extinguished by the dense gravity of her hyper-neediness.

The Bottomless Pit

This bottomless pit in a skirt is a drain on everyone's system. Women acquaintances do not like her because they cannot admire someone who depends so much on any one man for her validation as a person. They tire of her fixation on the guy of the moment and are bored because the new guy dominates every conversation. She does not focus on her female friends' lives, only on talking about every little detail of the current love of her life. When she shows up on a friend's doorstep after yet another rejection, she is inconsolable and after a while tries the patience of the listener. Friends finally say, "Get over it! Stop calling him so frequently! Pleading and begging him to take you back only makes him shy away from a bottomless pit that he will never be able to fill."

No Inner Resources

How did Needee Nellie get this way? Psychologists might say she has abandonment issues. Are you willing to hold her hand through countless therapy sessions in the hopes that she will overcome her fears? The point is, she is not good mate material right now. She does not have the inner resources to be a partner on an equal basis, someone who brings something to the relationship to make it worthwhile for you. A woman worthy of being a mate has a life of her own, interests of her own, and brings a love that comes from a strong center. She has goals for her life and wants to accomplish something other than being your parasite, sucking off of your life so she can fill her echoing chasms of emptiness.

A SOUL-SUCKER

Zilch, Goose-egg, Nada, Nothing

Like another of the Dirty Seven Sister discussed in this book, The Material Girl, Needee Nellie lives an empty life. But the Material Girl doesn't look to a man to fill her meaningless life with purpose. She finds meaning in material goods, self-grooming and shopping. The man is not the center of her life. She is more likely to use the man for what he can do for her financially. But Needee Nellie is like the cannibal who believes that in eating a human being, he is ingesting his soul. She wants your essence, or your actual life, to fill the empty space where her life is lacking. She will devote her days to sucking your soul from you to feed the hunger. The empty hole of her inner self is clamoring to be fed, fed, fed, like the plant in *The Little Shop of Horrors*. She will use whatever tactics to keep you with her because she is as desperate as the heroin addict in Needle Park needing the next fix.

Too Much, Too Soon

Needee Nellie often throws herself at a man early on in the relationship, even on the first date or encounter. She is not throwing herself at you because she is a sexually liberated woman who is using you as her boy toy. She flings herself at you to feed the hunger and desperation and to offer you some inducement to be interested in her. If you go for a second date with her, she may already pull up to your place in a U-Haul-It truck with all her belongings, ready to move in. A second date is like a marriage proposal to her. She will start her calling tactics after the first date but only two or three times a day the first week. After the second date she will give you romantic gifts that are not appropriate for your stage of the relationship and call you much more often.

Free Sex Samples
Do not get drawn in by her attempts to use sex to capture your interest. She knows that most men are not going to turn down a chance to get laid with a willing partner who will do anything they want in bed. Something in the back of your mind might be saying, "We've only known each other for a few hours and already she is letting me into her body cavities of all sorts. This isn't right!" But you might go through with it anyway, it is such a great opportunity for physical pleasure. You will pay the price later with her calls, instant messages on your computer, voicemail messages, and love notes left on your windshield, showing you that she has been following you around. "Why haven't you called me?", will be a frequent question in her messages. "I thought we had something really special! It was so romantic in the backseat of your car last night!"

Entrapping Tactics
One of Needee Nellie's entrapping tactics is to let you know how much she has done for you or how much money she has spent on gifts for you. You did not ask her to do or buy these things for you, but she will try to make you feel guilty enough about them to spend more time with her. She will cook, clean, and do every other domestic chore to make you

feel that she is indispensable in your life. What she is really doing is filling up her day with activity to keep from facing the emptiness inside. She is doing these things for you because she wants gratitude in the form of your undying commitment to be the meaning of her life. Whatever affection you might have initially felt for Needee Nellie will vanish as you realize that there is nothing there to the person whose manipulative tactics trapped you.

NEEDEE NELLIE MOMMIES

Baby, I Need Your Lovin'

Needee Nellies, because of their nurturing qualities appear to be great motherhood material. They are certainly more humane than the PMS Queens. But Needee Nellie needs to keep her babies as babies for life. Her dependent nature creates a scenario in which the children stay dependent on her, especially if she doesn't get enough of you. Since she never will get enough of you, due to her voracious need, she will make sure her children will become Mommy's Boys or Girls. Unless they completely rebel, they will not integrate well with other kids and will be seen as pampered, nerdy, dweeby, scairdy-cats.

She will be fearful of sending them away to school, camp, or even overnight to a sleepover at a friend's place. Her kids become her pals and they feel great guilt if they try to start a life of their own. When it is time for them to leave home she produces downpours of tears, "My baby is leaving me!" She will remind them constantly, "Call me every day!" If the kids get married, their new spouses will have to deal with her constant intrusion in their lives. This does not promise a happy life for your progeny, so think it over before you fall into the marshmallow sundae of Needee Nellie's love.

NEEDEE NELLIE EXAMPLES

Desperately Seeking. . . .

Vera wanted a man in her life so urgently, she might as well have worn a neon sandwich sign on her chest reading, "Desperately Seeking a Man, any Man will do." When she entered a mixed social gathering, her eyes anxiously scanned the room, looking for Mr. Right, Mr. Wrong, or Mr. Anything. Her eyes pierced into the face of any man who asked her to dance or who walked up to her for conversation. Most men could sense this clinginess and avoided her outright. So she pursued them and asked them to dance or initiated conversations, usually beginning with a compliment. Jay was one of her victims that night.

Vera was physically attractive, with her sparkling green eyes and glossy red hair. Jay found her friendliness and vulnerability appealing. She introduced herself early in the evening and stayed with him the entire night, talking and agreeing with practically everything he said. This was flattering, especially after a few drinks. It was a refreshing departure from the snooty, standoffish girls he had been meeting. As the hours passed, he felt he would have liked to talk to some of the other people in the room. The problem was that when he introduced himself to others or conversed with some of his friends, Vera tagged along and introduced herself too. It was almost as if they were a couple already!

When the party ended, she asked him to drive her home, since she arrived by taxi. Jay agreed and she reacted as if he just told her she won the lottery. As soon as she got into the car, she flung her arms around him and planted a huge, tongue-filled kiss on him. It was so full of saliva and passion, it was as if he had been a soldier missing in action in a foreign war, finally returning to his devoted fiancee. He barely got his key in the ignition when she took off her blouse.

She pounced on him, sticking her tongue down his throat. "I love you! I love you!", she howled as she began unbuttoning his shirt. "I have been looking for you all my life, and now I have found you! I need a man like you in my life!" She sprawled over him and squeezed like a boa constrictor, legs around his waist, all the while giving his tonsils a tongue-bath. The smoke alarm was going off in Jay's mind as he gasped for breath, but here was a girl offering herself up to him and it had been a long time since he had had sex. So he let her proceed with the sexual bonanza. He could blame it on the liquor later.

The next morning he woke up beside her in his bed. He didn't remember how this had happened or what went on, as his brain was still hazy from the booze. Her face was a quarter inch from his face and she was sucking the air out of his nostrils.

She looked into his eyes dreamily. "Wasn't last night great, My Love? It isn't very often that two soul mates find each other the way we have! I've fixed you breakfast, Honey!"

Breakfast came and went but she did not. She was still there for lunch. She needed a lot of affection and told him so, as if he couldn't see for himself. They spent the rest of the day in bed. Soon, but not soon enough, dinnertime came. She told Jay she wanted to have him over for dinner at her house. He was feeling leery about it, yet nevertheless agreed. At least it would be a way of getting her to go home. She did not have a car, he could not be so rude as to offer her money for a cab or bus, so he drove her to her place.

He waited there while she prepared an elaborate meal. The candles were glowing on the table. Potpourri scented the air. She had placed a wrapped gift by his plate. He opened it with slight trepidation before the meal. It was a star sapphire man's ring set in platinum. "It was my grandfather's favorite possession. I want you to have it," she said as she squirmed into his lap and smothered his face in kisses. "He was the greatest grandfather on earth and I know you are going to be the best boyfriend on earth!"

"Are you sure you want to give me such a precious possession?" Jay asked. "I mean, we have really only known each other less than 24 hours. I cannot take this. It wouldn't be right!" Vera looked hurt by this. Tears were forming in her eyes. She said, "No. I want you to have this. You mean so much to me already. I have the whole day tomorrow planned for us! I want you to meet my mother and father, then we will go over to my best friend's house, meet my favorite high school teacher, and then we will meet back to my place for dinner and more sex."

Jay had not planned for this and she was putting him on the

spot about the boyfriend issue. He told her he had other plans for the next day and she started sobbing. "My God, I hope you aren't like the other men I have been meeting. They are so commitment-phobic! You seemed different, so much better. Do this for me just this once. It would make me so happy!"

Jay excused himself and left, but that did not stop Vera from calling him a few times the next day. "What are you doing this weekend? I need someone to go to a wedding with me and I was also hoping we could visit my grandmother in the hospital together. On Sunday I've planned a trip to a day spa for His and Her massages! I miss you so much! I'm also planning a big house party to introduce you to my friends! By the way, what are you doing New Year's Eve? I have plans for us!"

"Whoa there, Nellie!" Jay replied. "I'm not ready for this kind of relationship. We had a nice time with each other, let's leave it at that. I still want to see other people and I also like to be alone sometimes."

Vera didn't hear him, apparently. She continued to leave messages on his answering machine. She sent him scenic, sentimental greeting cards. She wrote poems for him. She fired off several e-mail messages a day, telling him how completely enthralled she was with him. His ensuing silence made her morose: "I gave you my body, my soul, and my heart and you don't even return my calls! What have I done to deserve this kind of treatment from you? What kind of man are you, anyway? You men are all alike, you just use us and then toss us out like old Kleenex. Don't you know I can't live without you? I know, from our night of passion that you can't live without me either!"

He could and he did. He did not want to encourage her, so he was not home for her calls and left his answering machine on at all times, which she filled with messages. It took six months before all communication stopped from her. He felt relieved when he saw her at another party several months later. She was attached, leech-like, to another man's arm, looking up at him with cow-eyes, giving his face tongue baths, and planning for their future together.

Need-deep

Kathy and Damon had been going together since high school. Kathy went everywhere with her Damon, even to basketball games. These games bored her, but she couldn't stand being without him for more than a few hours. She tagged along when he had poker night with his friends. She even went on hunting trips with them and waited in the cabin all day for them to return. To make herself useful, she lugged provisions and prepared gourmet meals, so when they returned they wouldn't have to eat beef stew out of a can and wash it down with beer. She masterfully cooked such things as duck a' l' orange with steamed artichokes, ratatouille, and chocolate mousse, all with only two hotplates!

Damon had hinted to her that the men sometimes wanted to rough it and not be bothered with civilization. They wanted to sit around with each other and relax, not to worry about their language and behavior around her. They were becoming impatient with Damon's shadow and taunted him about it. He felt Kathy was boxing him into a corner, making him decide between her and his friends, because he knew she would find a way to be with him as much as possible. It hurt her feelings so much when he told her to cool it, and the hurt looks and tears were unsettling.

When he came home from work every night, he could see her silhouette on the curtain waiting by the window. She had read in one relationship book that a man wants the woman to greet him at the door tantalizingly wrapped in cellophane, ready to obey his every command and tried that too. Actually Damon wanted to command her to go away and give him a little time to himself. But, again, she was so sensitive, she cried easily and was readily hurt, so he tolerated her hovering efforts rather than see her despondent and uncomprehending.

One day Damon decided not to come home and went directly to a pub, where he and his friends were going to eat some hot wings, drink some brews, and hang out. Kathy drove all over town looking for him. She finally found where he was hiding and walked in with a face red and swollen with tears. She embarrassed Damon again, who already was taking a ribbing from the men about his Velcro girlfriend. "How could you do this to me?" Kathy sobbed. "I made a special dinner of everything you like and I have been slaving in the house all day long just to make it nice for you! Don't you know that I love you more than anything on earth? I would do anything for you, any time you want it! I gave you my life and all I am asking in exchange is yours!"

"Well, you're not going to get my life," Damon answered. "Tonight while I was away from you, I felt like I had just been let out of prison. You are a vampire. I can't breathe around you! It's like you're sucking the life-blood out of me! I hate to do this to you, but we're over. If I had a wooden cross, I'd wave it around to make you disappear. What do I have to do to get rid of you, drive a spike through your heart?"

Kathy answered, "You might as well drive a spike into my heart because I will never be able to live without you! You have killed me and now you have my death on your conscience!" She collapsed on the floor in a heap and shamelessly blubbered as Damon paid the tab and left without saying goodbye. After the discomfiture died down, all he could feel was relief. Her tears and protestations did not move him any more. He was finally free from the emotional bloodsucker whose name was Kathy.

I'll Change for You
Aisha could feel Tyreese slipping away. She thought it would be a good idea to search through his drawers, e-mail, and cell phone to see whom he might be seeing besides her. She followed him around on the sly, to see where he was going. Finding out what Tyreese was up to became the sole occupation of Aisha's life. She quit her job because it was preventing her from spending all her time on her detective work.

But she could find no evidence of another person taking her place in Tyreese's life. He was being true to her. That did not make her feel secure enough though, and soon she began to grill Tyreese. "Why do I feel that you are slipping away from me? Are you seeing someone else?" Tyreese did not want to tell her he was getting tired of her clinging ways. He wanted to avoid the inevitable wailing and gnashing of teeth he had seen in the past. But finally he blurted it out one night, after being exhausted from the constant questioning: "I have fallen out of love with you, Aisha. Things have changed between us. I feel you want something from me that I can't give you, namely, a life. I don't want to hurt your feelings about this, but I want to move out."

"Oh my God!" screamed Aisha. She was pulling at her hair, shaking and rocking. "Whatever it is about me that bothers you, I'll change! I already bought bigger boobs for you. I dyed my hair blonde because you mentioned one night that you liked blondes! I even let you bring another girl into the bedroom! How can you do this to me? I can't live without you! I am going to slit my wrists like the last time you said you were leaving! But this time I am going to cut much deeper so no one will be able to bring me back to life!"

Tyreese silently walked to the bathroom. He returned with a pack of razor blades and gently lay them on the table before he walked out.

NEEDEE NELLIE CELEBRITY EXAMPLES

Extreme Need
Most celebrities do not show their Needee Nellie qualities, if they have them, though many are driven to be celebrities

because of their intense need to be loved and validated by numbers of people. Their publicists do not allow them to display characteristics that point to lack of self-worth or make them appear desperate. However, you will notice a certain clinginess that some stars show in public as they hang all over their men. For example, some observers decry the way Melanie Griffith cling-wrapped herself around Antonio Banderas in public appearances, fearing he might escape if she had taken her eyes off him, even for a moment.

Melanie's Need

The venerable *National Enquirer,* which exposes the underbellies of the stars, reports on December 3, 2002:

"Antonio's had it! Melanie's become increasingly clingy during the six years they've been together, always pestering him over whether he's cheating on her and constantly seeking reassurances that he still loves her.

"She was beside herself with jealousy over Antonio's co-star in his new movie *Femme Fatale,* Rebecca Romijn-Stamos. Melanie grilled Antonio over whether he was having an affair with her.

"The irony is that Rebecca is about as safe a co-star as a man could have -- she's madly in love with her husband John Stamos, and like Antonio has no interest in cheating on her spouse.

"But Melanie can't get this fear that Antonio is cheating on her out of her head. Melanie's been in Australia playing Frank Sinatra's wife Barbara Marx in *The Night We Called*

It a Day. But being away hasn't helped the situation -- she worries constantly about what he's up to and calls and e-mails at all hours.

"Antonio finally told her one evening in a phone call that he couldn't take her jealousy anymore -- and that when she gets back to the States, he wouldn't be there to greet her.

"But the split isn't necessarily a death blow to the marriage -- Antonio's hoping that the move will help convince Melanie to rein in her jealousy.

"He's decided to step back and see if time and distance can help recapture their old passion.

"The fact is, Antonio loves Melanie, he loves his family life with her and their daughter Stella, and there have been no other women -- but he can't convince her that he has eyes only for her.

"He's decided to stay away for a few weeks to let her sort through things and to let him sort through things as well.

"He feels Melanie needs to get a grip, and he's hoping that leaving will bring her around and make her stop being so clingy. But there's no guarantee this isn't the end! "

"The 45-year-old actress' insecurities stem from 'low self-esteem' and her fear that Antonio, 42, will fall for a younger woman, an insider revealed.

"Melanie has such low self-esteem that when she looks in

the mirror she doesn't see what everyone else sees. To her, she is a woman struggling to keep her dashing husband.

"Melanie believes Antonio could have his pick of any younger woman he wants and she fears he's going to leave her for a woman who can give him another child.

"'Melanie knows how much Antonio wants another child and has been beating herself up over the fact she's not been able to get pregnant again,' said a close family friend.

"She has been undergoing fertility treatments, injecting herself with hormones and visiting a fertility specialist on a regular basis.

"But she's not been able to give Antonio a son. She's a wreck.

"She's been on the phone constantly, calling everyone she knows and asking what she can do to win Antonio back.

"Antonio helped Melanie through rehab recently, and he still loves her. And he's certain that if she can pull herself together just a little, they can make it over the long haul."

Angelina's Need

The way Angelina Jolie flew across the country to obtain a fresh vial of Billy Bob Thornton's blood verges on the psychotically needy. On April 4, 2001, *The New York Post* reported that Angelina showed up to a photo shoot wearing a glass ball pendant containing drops of Billy Bob Thornton's blood and when asked to remove it for the shoot she refused, telling her assistant, "This is my husband's blood! If there was a safe way I could drink his blood, I'd love to." She also bought a couple of burial plots to celebrate their first anniversary. During a ceremony to renew their marriage vows, they cut each other's fingers and sipped away at each other s blood. Finally, when she played Lara Croft in *Tomb Raider*, she insisted her character needed an electric chair in her room because, "Billy got electrocuted in a movie this year, so it was romantic for me to have it."

Angelina once said she broke down on a movie set "screaming about how much I wanted him. I also have this thing about his earlobe," she told a reporter. I just want to bite it off so many times."

Is it any wonder that both actors did their best work playing mental patients, she in *Girl, Interrupted*, he in *Sling Blade*? Now the couple is no longer together and their marriage, as performance art, came to an abrupt halt.

Meg and Russell
The print media have made much of Meg Ryan's purported obsession with Russell Crowe. She supposedly sent over 200 e-mail messages and made countless phone calls to revive their relationship after their split. This kind of neediness borders on harassment and usually backfires into driving the man away. She said she felt "empty and adrift" after her bust-up with Crowe. On April 1, 2001 she sounds like she is climbing out of the abyss of need with a new awareness: "I was feeling empty, like a ship without an anchor. A friend of mine told me I felt that way because I

didn't have a man in my life, and it just opened up my eyes. Why are women always seen and labeled according to the man they're with? The most important man in my life right now is my son - and that's how I'm keeping it." (Source WENN 4/1/01).

That resolution did not last long. On April 16, she was already reportedly flirting with Tim Robbins. An eyewitness says, "Meg was acting like a smitten schoolgirl, gazing into Tim's eyes, laughing at everything he said and grabbing his hand to let him know how terribly amusing she found every word he said."

Meg told a friend, "Tim is a woman's dream, he is mature, intelligent and funny. You just want to wrap him up and take him home." Weeks later she reportedly tried to win Crowe back, spent the night with him in New York City and was devastated once more when he left to fly to Fiji for a vacation with Nicole Kidman.

PREVENTION: DO NOT BE FOOLED

All Sizes and Shapes

Needee Nellies come in all sizes and shapes. You might think that only the most unattractive women could be so desperate for a man. But this is not so. As with the celebrity examples above, a beautiful woman can be needy and clingy too. She lures a man in through her appearance, which she owes to nature's generosity and cosmetic arts. She may feel insecure because she knows she has not earned her positive endowments, so she needs constant reassurance. Her beauty can fade or become twisted by the continuous demands she places on you to prove to her that you love her. Her beauty may even become a bit obnoxious, when you realize how stupid you were for falling for it. Inner neediness is no respecter of persons. It cuts across all types of women. Educated or ignorant, well bred or lowly, her blood-sucking lack of personhood wears out the man who endures it.

Nicey-nice
Be careful about the initial sweetness of Needee Nellie. She is a bit nicer than most people are from the start, showing you right away how accommodating she is. She is certainly no Tantrum-Diva PMS Queen. As with all the Dirty Seven Sisters, what starts out as potentially fascinating ends up being a disaster. Talk with the woman before you sleep with her or think you are in love with her. Does she seem too nice to be for real? Does she agree with everything you say and stare at you as if you were the apotheosis of greatness, her hero?

Does She Have a Life?
If you believe in love at first sight, force yourself to step back and take the time to have several conversations with the object of your desire before plunging into the river of sexual ecstasy with her. See if she has a life or if she is waiting around for someone to lend her his life. If she does not have a life, she might be like the aliens in the film *The Invasion of the Body Snatchers*. Your life may be ripe for the picking. Many a man has confided to me that he has fallen in love with some glorious creature who feeds his fantasy of what he wants in a woman. He is willing to jump

into a relationship quickly because he wants to have a good time and is attracted and interested. But the good times will come to a messy end when the fantasy dies and Cinderella turns into Vampira, feeding on his life so she can sustain her own.

Do Not Be Flattered

It can be flattering when a women dwells on your every word as if it were manna from heaven and looks into your eyes as if you were the savior of mankind. If you have been lonely for too long, the constant companionship that Needee Nellie requires seems cozy to you. But like a downy quilt on a steamy summer day, her smothering inability to be on her own, for even a short time, will suffocate you in its warmth. Do not be so quick to be flattered by an unknown lady's attentions, especially if she is coming on too strong, too fast. Take charge of your inner ape and use the judgment of a rational man who has evolved out of the jungles of impulse and shortsightedness. Walk away from the quicksand before it engulfs you!

MATERIAL GIRL

SKIN DEEP

All Surface
Needee Nellies, as you now know, feel empty inside and want you to fill them up. Material Girls do not feel empty inside because they do not think enough to feel empty. They are indeed empty inside but are so unreflecting, they do not even know that they are vacuous. Furthermore, they do not even care that they are shallow. They love themselves just the way they are, all surface and no substance. They cannot imagine any other way of being.

Three Varieties
Material Girls come in three varieties:

- **Gimmie Monie:** You are a walking dollar bill whose purpose is to support her in a life of luxury.
- **Prettie Pennie:** Spends all her time and energy on self-beautification and adornment; the lights are on but nobody's home.
- **Thingie Wingie:** Spends her days acquiring things, talking about things, shopping for things, exchanging things, and maintaining things. May be a workaholic to support this activity.

GIMMIE MONIE

Give Me!
Gimmie Monie's motto comes from the Beatles' song whose title is her life's obsession: Money. "Money can't buy everything it's true, but what it don't get, I can't use. Gimme money, that's all I want."

Cold-heart
She is not interested in you unless you provide her with lots of money. If you do, she will be charming. But do not think she wants the companionship and love you offer, especially if your wallet is not packed with the real object of her affection. Gimmie Monie does not believe in love, except self-love, not that she reflects on the subject much. Her heart is as cold and hard as a silver dollar on ice. If your gravy train does not make it into the station, she will hop the next one out of town. She has no loyalty except to her pursuit of wealth and its display. Her calculating brain rings like a cash register when she zeros in on her prey.

Show Me the Money
"You give it to me. I take it," sums up her attitude. "I want a life of leisure, with all the perks, while you battle it out in the world to get these things for me." Somehow she feels entitled to this bounty. Isn't she letting you into her secret garden? Isn't that enough? She considers herself quite a prize. She might brag to her friends, "I only date inter-national business types." She is direct in her requirements and usually asks a man on the first date how much money he makes. If he objects and does not answer, or answers but does not make enough, she excuses herself to go the lady's

room and walks out.

What are You Worth?
Her date might say, "This isn't fair! She isn't even giving a man a chance. I have earning potential and everyone knows I'm a nice guy. Just because I told her how much I'm making now, she walks out on me?" Yes. The person is secondary to the money. If you do not have it, she feels she is wasting her time on her way to her goal: To meet and marry Money. The fact that there is a man attached to The Money is an inconvenience she has to put up with to get what she wants. She will tolerate sex, time together, and even meeting your family if you can give her what she wants. Then, if things do not work out, she will slap you with the maximum in alimony, palimony, and other compensations for putting in her time with you.

The Alimony Pit
Some Gimmie Monies diligently wait for their prey because they know exactly what they want out of life: Marriage, divorce within a reasonable time, and the pay-off, alimony. They are as single-minded in this goal as patient spiders spinning their webs to catch their evening's dinner. Like black widow spiders, devouring their mates as post-coital snacks, they know what they want and have no scruples about getting it.

My friend Earline is an example of the Alimony Gimmie Monie-style woman. She noticed that an elderly man had taken an interest in me. "Why don't you go out with him?", she prodded. I told her we had nothing in common and I was not interested in him in that way. She said, "You could get him to marry you, get divorced, and be set up for the rest of your life. He's crazy about you, haven't you noticed? Have you seen his properties? I'd jump at this one in a minute! You're a fool! I've been waiting for a chance like this for a long time!" I told her if I wanted to sell myself, I'd be a call girl. "You can still be that if you want to and keep milking him too, Silly! The alimony payments would set you up for life!"

The More Honorable Prostitute

After reading the above, you might ask yourself, "What is the difference between Gimmie Monie and the average prostitute?" The answer is, with a prostitute the transaction is straightforward. You pay money, she sells you sex. No pretense of emotional involvement or love comes into play. With Gimmie Monie you pay and pay and you still might not get sex, depending how she feels and what else she wants out of you. She also pretends to love you to get what she wants. In this light, the prostitute is a better bargain and more honorable, though her conduct is illegal and she can go to jail for it. As underhanded as it is, Gimmie Monie's behavior is perfectly within the law.

World Wide Web

The term World Wide Web takes on new meaning when applied to the traps some Gimmie Monies weave. Admittedly, you deserve what you get when you go on the Internet to find a wife. If you are willing to marry a woman, sight and behavior unseen, you are asking for it. The attractive women you see are trading their beauty, companionship, and sex to get out of a country where they live a deprived lifestyle and have a limited future. Do you honestly think the woman will love you because you have helped her get citizenship? Get real! Love is not something traded for something else. It is spontaneous and mysterious, not something you plan. She might show gratitude the way a stray dog feels on an stormy night when you take it in, but do not even count on that either.

The Price of Motherhood
Children of Gimmie Monies learn early that everything has a price tag on it. Nothing is free, including love and affection. They use money and things as rewards for good behavior, rather than stressing that good behavior has its own rewards. The up-side to this is they teach their kids about the value of a dollar. But as role models, people who put cash above love on their priority list do not offer the nurturing qualities children need.

Gimmie Monies remind their children about all the money they have spent on them. They may start charging their kids rent before they are of age to leave home. If they counsel their kids on careers, it will be for some work that brings in lots of cash, as opposed to a humanitarian calling. They will screen their kids' future mates for cash potential. The kids may grow up thinking that money is the meaning of life and accumulating it is the reason for living.

PRETTIE PENNIE

Lights on, Nobody Home
A beautiful, well-groomed woman is a pleasure, especially when her beauty reflects her personality and individuality.

But Prettie Pennie has neither personality nor individuality. She is like Gertrude Stein's Oakland, California, "There's no there, there!" She looks good, but that's about it. She is all surface, with nothing going on underneath. She has the depth of single-ply tissue. She works at perfecting that surface to the exclusion of everything else. She is like a beautiful house, which as you get closer, you discover is empty inside. Lights are blazing from the sparkling chandeliers, but nobody's home.

Veneer-deep

She has figured out that appearances attract but that is as far as her powers of analysis go. She devotes the rest of her thoughts and all her money, plans, and time on making herself gorgeous. She spends long hours at the beauty salon getting those highlights, streaks, and chunks just right. She devotes many hours a week getting pedicures, manicures, facials, waxes, and massages. When she is not self-grooming she is exercising and tanning. She spends the rest of the time reading and talking about self-beautification. The day does not contain enough hours to take care of her beauty needs. Dire human events may happen around her but they do not touch her, unless they get in the way of her beauty rituals. She is a survivalist when it comes to preserving the veneer.

Looking Good

Looking good is important to most healthy people for a number of reasons. It shows we care about the way we face the day. Being well groomed indicates high self-esteem. Psychiatrists note that lack of self-care is a symptom of psychological difficulties. Beyond showing a sense of self-worth, balanced women groom themselves to be effective in their lives and careers. The problem with Prettie Pennie is that grooming is not a means to an end; it is an end in itself. It is her life and her career; her whole reason for living. She does not think beyond it. Everything she does is in support of her goal: Self-beautification, which takes a lifetime to achieve as she eternally battles the forces of gravity and entropy.

Alluring Illusion

You may meet her at a nightclub or ballgame, where the sound is loud and there is a lot of activity, thus eliminating the need for conversation of any importance. She is sexy-looking and dressed in a way that grabs your attention. But if you spend some time getting to know her, you will see that she is not sexual or sensual at all. She got herself up that way to present the illusion of being alluring because that is the fashion of the day. Besides, how else can she attract a sugar daddy so she doesn't have to put in time at that boring job -- time she could be spending shopping at the mall? In actuality, she does not want you to mess up her hair and makeup by getting too physical with her. She spends hours achieving that look and does not want to destroy it with your body fluids! Besides, your kisses are painful to her newly collagen-implanted lips.

Don't Mess up My Do!

She spends a lot of money and time to create the illusion of a sexual being: Bee-stung lips, hair streaked and tousled to create the appearance of a day at the beach or making love, eyes expertly made up to look like a lusty vixen, Wonder-bra'd chest spilling out over a flimsy tube top. But do not get too close. She will be upset with you if you mess her up too much by running your hands through her hair. And do not be messing up her makeup! Besides, making love with you might interfere with her workout at the gym. She cannot give her all to both, so guess who gets put on the back burner? If she feels like it, she might lie there and let you get it over with, while she thinks about changing her nail polish to that new color everyone is wearing this season. Should she splurge and get the Chanel or the drugstore look-alike?

Nixon Who?

Because Prettie Pennie's entire brain is engaged in the process of self-adornment, she has not had much time for reading or any other activity that requires thinking. Therefore, do not expect to have any meaningful conversation with her about the basic issues of life. Even on a getting-to-know-you basis, conversation is limited. She describes some of her activities, but never her thoughts or feelings about anything of greater weight than if she should go curly or straight this week. If you try to talk to her about current events, or history, you see that she doesn't have a clue about any of it. For example, if you mention Watergate and President Nixon, she might ask, "Wasn't he the man in that movie about those guys in suits who did something or other? I think one of the men needed a shave?" When you explain, her eyes glaze over. She is not interested and never will be.

Prettie Pennie's Progeny

Children of Prettie Pennie feel she resents them because they ruined Mom's figure when they made their appearance in this world. She will remind them of this often, especially if they get her annoyed. "I was so hot before you came along and spoiled my beautiful body forever. Look at this stretch mark! I never got my hips back to where they were before you came along!"

Prettie Pennie hates herself when her body is distorted by pregnancy and takes great pains to stay fashion-thin during this time, regardless of its effect on the baby. She starves herself to make sure she does not go over her pre-pregnancy weight, which was already low. How she looks is so important, she makes sure she is wearing makeup during labor and delivery. She might reject the baby, who when it first appears, is wrinkled and discolored. She had been nursing the fantasy of a pink-cheeked charmer from a baby food jar label and didn't expect this frog-like being that creates such a mess and is wailing away unattractively, searching for food.

THINGIE WINGIE

Thing-aholic
Thingie Wingie is the woman who spends all her thoughts and time on buying, exchanging, and thinking about the consumer goods she wants and the status she thinks they reflect upon her. She thinks buying, shopping, and name brands are the only interesting topics of conversation. Her conversation about her new Beamer gets highly animated, as she blindly believes that everyone has bought into her value system. Somehow, the fact that she has exchanged money for some object or another gives her self worth. She

also wants to show the world she has value, so she is quick to point out her recent acquisitions. She thinks everyone is as fascinated with the symbols she covets, whether they are the latest watches or the biggest lawns to mow, including the status lawnmower. She is so blind to other purposes in life, she thinks everyone is devoting their lives to getting these things too.

Thingolatry

Thingie Wingie is an empty shell, like Prettie Pennie. The difference is that she is not as obsessed with making herself gorgeous as she is with objects outside herself. Material objects are the center of her life and conversation. She might be like Violette, whom I met at a party. After saying introductory hellos she trotted out photos of her huge new house and lawn. She wanted to impress me with how many hours she spent every summer weekend harvesting her mammoth grass crop and maintaining her castle full of bathrooms. Her reverence and worship of these things are what I call, "thingolatry." Things have taken the place of the inner core of personhood. Like the devout worshipper at the statue of her God, she lights a candle to the object of her reverence: Things.

The Brand is Right

If you are looking for someone who has an inner life, pass on Thingie Wingie. You can pick her out easily by noticing her conversation. Notice how she avoids thoughts and ideas. Notice also, that she is not interested in you, but rather in what you are wearing, your car, and things that someone else has created and you have bought. Her conversation sounds something like this:

TW: I like your jacket. It looks like a Perry Ellis. I got something like that for my brother for his birthday. I didn't know what to get him, the Perry Ellis or the Nautica, but I like this new greenish brown.

You: Thanks. You have a brother?

TW: Your shirt is cool too. Is it a Tommy knockoff? I don't see his name on it anywhere. I saw something like it at Nordie's yesterday in the woman's section but it had a thinner red stripe across the upper back and a big block of blue on the sleeve. I was there to get a Coach purse for my mom's birthday. I spent half the day in line taking back the Fendi I bought her because she already had something like it.

You: Yesterday was a beautiful day! Too bad you spent so much of it indoors shopping.

TW: Hey, shopping is my life!

You: What about other stuff going on in the world? Like, what do you think about the oil situation? Do you think we are getting closer to easing dependency on fossil fuels?

TW: Are you talking about the new Fossil watches? I almost got one the other day. It was a toss-up between that and the Swatch! I want something different from the Tag Hauer I just bought.

Endless Stuff

The shallow Thingie Wingie has little capacity for feeling and thought, though her mind is not empty like Prettie

Pennie's unfurnished rooms. ThingieWingie's mind is a room overstuffed with things that crowd all thoughts and people out. Because her greatest excitement is reserved for objects, not people, if you marry her, her conversations with you consists mostly of things to buy. Her conversation with friends who stop by is about the lawn, its furniture; the house, its furnishings, and possibly the status vacations she documents and collects with the intent to impress. Most of the fun time you spend with her is in the stores buying more stuff for the house. What will you learn from her? Where to buy what, what's the latest status symbol, and who has it. The rest is useless chatter on how she spent her day taking care of Things.

Thingie Wingie and Workaholism

Thingie Wingie is different from Gimmie Monie because she doesn't necessarily depend on you to give her money to buy all the things she craves. She is willing to go out and earn the money herself but might be a workaholic because of this. You might want to take her out but she is working late again. She works late every night and sometimes on weekends. It's not because she is doing important work that is fulfilling to her soul and beneficial to mankind. She is making more money to accomplish her latest goal, to buy the Vuitton luggage set she has been coveting for weeks. If you marry her, prepare for an absent wife. This might be a relief from her empty chatter but is no substitute for a warm, loving, affectionate mate who cares about people instead of things.

Miss Thing's Kiddies

Children of Thingie Wingies tend to feel that the living

room furniture is more important than they are. Their homes are museums in which they can look at things but must not touch. They learn soon that they are messy creatures that dangerously hover on the verge of dirtying the items on display and incurring their guardian's wrath. They spend their young lives learning to be consumers like Momma Thingie Wingie, going to malls and department stores, shopping and talking about shopping, maintaining and worshipping things. Children adapt well to the positive rewards they get for being just like Mommy and can either become good little carbon copies or rebel completely and become hippies who renounce all the trappings of the status-seeking world.

MATERIAL GIRL EXAMPLES

The Color of Money

Roland met Jasmina one night at a singles' get-together. She was beautiful on the moonlit night they kissed. Her story was so sad. She was from a third-world country with many brothers and sisters. Her mother was sick and needed a simple operation to save her life. But her family didn't have the money. Her brothers and sisters didn't even have shoes to wear to school.

Roland offered to help. He saw that he could easily pay for her mother's operation. He even gave Jasmina an extra thousand dollars to get her brothers and sisters shoes, clothes, and supplies for school.

It was a pleasure for Roland and Jasmina loved him so

much. She told him so several times a day. She wasn't demanding like some of the women of the modern world he had known from his past.

She was soft and appealingly passive. They got married and Roland continued sending money to her family every month. Now that they were married, Jasmina, though sweet, was frequently ill. He understood she had been malnourished and sometimes didn't want to have sex. Roland was an understanding person about these things. She was his wounded bird and he was taking care of her.

Roland's office closed early one day and he unexpectedly went home. His face turned the color of money as he stood at the bedroom door. On their marriage bed was Jasmina noisily speaking her language as she engaged in sex with a man of her same nationality. They were so intent on each other they didn't notice Roland standing there.

The true story came out. His loving Jasmina had used the money he gave her to fly her boyfriend over and set him up in a nearby apartment. They usually got together there. Today was an exception. Later Roland found letters he wrote to Jasmina, congratulating her on luring their prey. A few of them prompted her to tell him how much she loves him, several times a day.

Killer Looks

Tom was looking forward to a day with Heather on the beach. When he met her, he was struck with her beauty. She was quiet, but that only added to her mystery. Besides, he couldn't stand women who talked too much. It was enough just to be with her and bask in her beauty.

She was stunning lying on the sand, with her smooth, even tan. She told him she had been hitting the tanning booth for days just in preparation for today but she was also using a self-tanner as backup. They baked in the sun in silence. The lack of conversation began to feel awkward to Tom. He wanted to get to know her better. But any time he introduced a subject, he got a "yes" or "no" answer with nothing after it. Sometimes when he phrased a question that required more than a no or yes answer, her questions showed a disturbing lack of knowledge of the most elementary things. For example, when he told her about his trip to Arizona, she said, "That's somewhere in Spain, isn't it, or is it that yummy ice-tea drink?"

He suggested they go for a swim. She looked at him like he was an escaped lunatic. "You don't really think I was going to spend all morning on my makeup and hair, so the whole thing could be destroyed by one second in the water, do you?" Tom went off to swim by himself. He saw other girls laughing and swimming in the water, enjoying the day. He looked up on the beach and saw his Pretty Princess Heather reading a magazine. Good! The magazine would give them something to talk about.

He approached their blanket with admiration in his eyes for her beauty. Drops of water glistened on his skin. "Don't get near me!" Heather squealed. "I don't want you to mess up my self-tanner with sea water! It always gets blotchy on me when I get near salt water!"

"What are you reading?" Tom asked, to divert the subject. She showed him. It was a fashion magazine. She let him stand there while she pointedly ignored him, deeply engrossed in the glossy pages. Finally she pointed to a model. "Do you think she's prettier than I am?" Tom felt he was suddenly treading in dangerous waters. He knew he couldn't say "yes." That would be a complete disaster. So he said, "No, you're prettier."

"Well, what about her?" she asked, pointing to another one. For the rest of the afternoon, this was all she wanted to do, ask him about each model in the magazine and be reassured that she was prettier than all of them. Finally Tom decided that this was enough. Being with this beauty was downright boring! When she pointed to the next model and asked the question, he said disgustedly, "No, she's prettier than you are. Her breasts are bigger. Her skin is clearer."

Heather began to cry and told him she hated him. The tears were messing up her mascara and her eyes were burning! What a rip-off. The lady at the cosmetics counter told her it was waterproof! The world sucked! How could he do this to her? Now she probably looked like a dismal raccoon because he made her cry. She could have been getting a facial instead of wasting her time with him today!

She took the magazine and slammed it over his head, giving him a paper cut near his eye. Oh no! She broke a nail! "Oh my God! Take me home now!" she sobbed. Her magazine was torn on the page with that important new article on those 18-hour lipsticks. "I could kill you and no one would blame me. It's all your fault! You better buy me a new magazine too! And to think I wasted a deluxe pedicure on a jerk like you!" She rode all the way home in silence, nursing her broken claw with the tenderness of a new mother.

Hey, You, Get offa My Couch

Darlene fell in love the moment she walked into Bloomies' furniture showroom and saw her dream couch. There it sat in its dazzling glory, inspiring, almost religious, in its intense thing-ness. When she saw its price she was shocked but set her jaw with visionary vigor. She had to have it at any cost and she would work overtime if she had to get it!

Weekends and nights, while others were out relaxing and having fun, she was pursuing her dream beneath the fluorescent lights of her office. Finally she made enough in overtime to buy her ticket to paradise. So you can imagine how upset she was when her husband Doug wanted to make love last night on it! She was disgusted with him about a lot of things these days, but this was the final outrage. He spilled some water on the new hardwood floor and didn't clean it up right away, broke one of her treasured Royal Doultons while doing the dishes Saturday night, and was wearing off-brand clothes far too much these days. Now he actually wanted to risk getting bodily fluids all over the lush, sensuous fabric of her most beloved object!

The choice was obvious. Doug had to go! She neared the couch. Oh no! Doug was sitting on it drinking a glass of wine! "Doug, what in the hell do you think you're doing?" She screamed until her vocal chords rasped.

Doug, who had been sitting peacefully sipping his wine and

reading, jolted, alert with shock. Oh God! She startled him! Some of the wine splashed over the rim of the glass onto the creamy, awe-inspiring fabric of the armrest. The red lines of her veins stood out in her eyes, which were overflowing with tears as she quavered, "I never want to see you again! We're history! It's over Doug!"

Darlene thought she was on the verge of a medical emergency, her choking sobs were so severe she couldn't breathe! Her couch! She couldn't believe he had the nerve to even sit on it, no less have a glass of wine on it! It was like desecrating the holy shrine of the Supreme Deity! Now she was going to devote her life to finding out how to remove wine stains and restore her darling to its pristine loveliness. She could hear Doug close the door as he left for good. Good! Now she and her treasure could be alone, together in peace.

The Gift Horse's Mouth

Misty opened the pale robin's-egg-blue box. Her look of delight changed to dismay. Ricardo was hurt. What was wrong? He had just spent $6,500 on the gold mesh bracelet with the clasp of Tiffany diamonds set in platinum. He had been saving for this for a year. He had been dreaming about how her smile would illuminate her gorgeous features as she radiated pleasure at his gift of love. But she was crying instead of smiling and her face was distorted with emotion. Her tears gave him a lump of happiness in his throat. He knew her heart had been set on this masterpiece of craftsmanship for a long time.

Finally Misty spoke, "Ricardo, I can't believe you did this!"

Tears were now carving pale rivulets through the makeup on her cheeks. "You know I had my heart set on the Jean Schlumberger fringe necklace with the 50 round brilliant cut diamonds. I can't believe you didn't remember that!" Ricardo gulped for air. "That little beauty costs $39,250!"

"You were always cheap, Ricardo. I know for a fact that Amy is getting the Schlumberger pearl collar and Jeremy isn't batting an eye at its $195,000 price tag," she said petulantly.

Ricardo snatched the box and bracelet out of her hands and walked away disgusted. He was tired of this heartless little platinum-digger and disappointed with how she returned his care and kindness. A diamond was softer than her heart! It wasn't enough for her that he supported her completely in her life of ease, she wanted more and more. She was out lunching with her lady friends and getting massages while he was fighting it out in the city in his business, thinking he was creating a good life for both of them. Now he had to think about how he was going to get out of the marriage. He knew she would try to soak him for a big chunk of his income. He would be tied to her for life with invisible chains of cash as she drained his earnings out of him, like a faucet dripping blood, one painful drop at a time.

Show Me the Alimony!
These are Jim's own words about his Material Girl experience: "Well, I have a pretty crappy situation, in my opinion. I am twenty-two years old and have already been married and divorced, and have a three year old daughter. I would be able to write a book on all the bull my ex has put

me through and although I'm not saying I was perfect, I gave everything I could to my ex, Janey, and she really screwed me over.

"We just got our divorce, which she filed for, about two months ago and she has been living with her new boyfriend for about the same amount of time, (with my daughter, my furniture, and brand new washer and dryer, mind you) and I was ordered to pay child support. I have no problem supporting my daughter financially, and I want to be there for her emotionally as well. I wouldn't even be in this state if I didn't want to be here for my daughter. Anyway, I feel I was a little screwed by the court. I was awarded joint custody, thankfully, but was barely awarded any real visitation, the court said it was due to her age, and was ordered to pay $466.00 a month for one child.

"I live in Arizona, and have been told that the basic whole support for one child, according to state standards, is $520. Which is saying that if the mother doesn't work, that's what you would have to pay to support that child. But in reality, Janey is now living in a really nice home with her new boyfriend, and my new furniture, drives a new car, and works full time. So I am left with the hefty bills while she is enjoying her life with her new boyfriend!"

Money Matters
Here is another true account, as told by Rupert: "I've dated many women, some seriously, and others for pure sexual pleasure. But I've never come across a woman who absolutely refused to pay for anything with her own money like Rosa -- my girlfriend of eight months.

"I don't mind paying for the date, but the problem is she has a very expensive taste. Let me give you an example: Rosa likes to go out to fancy restaurants, at least once a week and it usually costs me $200 a night. As you can imagine, it can get quite expensive, and this does not include gifts, parking, movies, plays, and so on.

"The reason I've tolerated her exploitation up to this point is because Rosa has an angel-like model face, and curves that would put the sensual Czech model, Veronica Varekova, to shame.

"However, Rosa recently did something that was the last straw. Two weeks ago, she decided to get some fast food and because it was her idea and cheap, I was expecting Rosa to foot the bill. But before getting out of the house, she asked me for $40 in order to pay for the meal.

"Here's the kicker: I know for a fact that the meal did not cost more than $15, and Rosa had the gall to keep the change! At this point, I was infuriated. Not only was she a gold digger, but she was also a moneygrubber. That explains why she didn't pay for dinner on my birthday -- even after she invited me.

"So now I'm debating here, why should I stick around? If she's in the relationship for the money, then I may as well get someone else. Yes I know, she does have a beautiful face and a great body, but at what cost?"

CELEBRITY MATERIAL GIRL EXAMPLES

Anna's Sugar Daddy

Not too many people believed that the 30-year-old Anna
Nicole Smith married her 90-year-old husband because of
his fabulous personality and amatory skills. He met her at a
strip bar and probably knew exactly what she was after. But
he was happy with it anyway. He probably figured he might
as well enjoy the few months he had left to live. His family
was outraged at the $450 million she got at his passing.

Joanie Dearest

Joan Crawford, with her, "No wire hangers!" rampage is an
excellent example of Thingie Wingie, for whom objects are
more important than people. Her daughter alleges that
Joan beat her with the wire hangers in outrage that her
closet should contain such an abomination. Her child's
bruised and battered body was not as important as having
wooden and satin hangers for her clothes. The men in Joan's
life were steppingstones to her career advancement,
expendable as the wire hangers she couldn't tolerate.

Bonnie

Bonnie Lee Bakely, the star stalker, was a grifter who
played confidence games on men to elicit money. In 1998,
she was caught in Arkansas with seven driver's licenses and
five Social Security cards, all registered in different
names. She was a groupie, one who followed the trail of
men in the entertainment media. She spun tales to her
family and friends of her intimate relationships with
second-string celebrities such as Jerry Lee Lewis and
Frankie Valli, who nevertheless had money she could spend.

Her stated goal to everyone in earshot was to marry a music or movie star. She kept a diary on her tactics for putting herself in the path of selected celebrities and studied their movements and whereabouts at certain times of the day and night. In 2000, she finally landed the Hollywood husband she had always hoped for, Robert Blake, after managing to get pregnant with his baby.

By several accounts Bonnie was married nine times. Investigators are looking into the fact that she may have been married up to a hundred times, and that none of these marriages may have been valid at all.

Bonnie moved to Tennessee to be close to singer Jerry Lee Lewis, whom she pursued with fervor. Attending rock concerts and cozying up to male celebrities, Bonnie made dozens of well-connected friends. She named her third child Jeri Lee Lewis, claiming that Jerry Lee Lewis was the child's father.

Bonnie met Robert Blake at a Hollywood party in 1999 after staking him out and studying his habits. When she became pregnant, she believed that Christian Brando was the father, according to Blake's lawyers. It didn't matter to her, as long as fame, money, and celebrity were involved. But after the baby was born, a DNA test confirmed that the child was Blake's and Bonnie claimed the conception happened during her first sexual encounter with him.

They married, even though Blake was suspicious of her and was fighting alcoholism and depression. He hired investigators to look into her background, which was shady with arrests, prosecutions, and confirmed incidents of bilking men for cash. She had announced to her family that her aim in life was to be "the female Donald Trump" but she was just another Material Girl looking to get rich quick. She got rich and dead, quick.

PREVENTION: CONVERSATION PIECES

Knock, Knock, Who's There?

I cannot emphasize enough that you must go against your genetic impulse to mate with the best-looking woman in the room. Show those genes who's boss! Beauty does not equal goodness, kindness, thoughtfulness, fun, a sense of humor, or depth. Beauty does not mean she will be a good mother to your children. Find out what is going on inside the head of that Venus Flytrap before your fly gets caught in her trap. If you explore her mind and heart and discover only consumer goods, cosmetics, and money, pass her by.

SHOPAHOLICA

SHE SHOPS 'TIL YOU DROP

Greener Pastures
Shopaholica is the girl who is with you, but is really looking for someone better. In the meantime, she will keep you on the string until Mr. Right comes along. She never gives her heart because she is keeping it in reserve for him, but will still spend time with you and act like she is your girlfriend. Or, maybe she is already attached and you are her next potential Mr. Right, so she will cultivate you while keeping her other man on the string. As complicated as this sounds, it is really quite simple: She is never in the present moment, enjoying the now with you, because she is holding out for someone she can really love. Greener pastures are just over the horizon for her and they are not with you, here and now. Nevertheless, if you are like some hopeful men, you might make the mistake of hanging around. You will wait patiently until the day she will discover that your pasture is the one she wants to graze in after all, won't she?

Mr. Next
Actually, Shopaholica is not looking for Mr. Right. She is looking for Mr. Next. She gets bored easily. She does not have the patience to work on a relationship or cut you a little slack if you break her rules of life. A few slip-ups, according to her rules of life, and you are definitely out of the running. What are her rules of life? They keep changing, so do not even try to comprehend them. She will keep you around for a booty call though, so if you are happy with that

for the time being, go for it. While you are eating dinner with her on a date, her eyes might be scanning the room for a potential Mr. Next. She might even show the waiter a little more attention that he deserves for pouring water in her glass. But she will accept your gifts, let you pick up the tab, let you take her on expensive dates, and have you pick her up at the airport at two in the morning on her way back from seeing another Mr. Next in another city.

Just Looking

Novelty is more important to Shopaholica than depth of experience with one person. But she is not as shallow as the Material Girl. She might be able to carry on a conversation on a wide range of subjects and show a mind capable of analysis, with refreshing, original opinions. If you are looking for an interesting experience you might want to stay with her. Forget it though, if you are looking for intimacy. She is not intellectually shallow, just emotionally lacking, at least towards you. You are a way station on the path to her final destination. She does not know what the destination is, except that you are not it. You can hang on until she figures it out, if you want to. But recognize that she is just window-shopping to kill time until the real thing comes along.

Dating Around

At this point you might be saying, "It just sounds like she is dating around. What's wrong with that? It's smart to try out different people before you settle down." The difference between what Shopaholica does and just dating around is that if a date doesn't work out, she still keeps him on a string anyway, because he may be useful to her. According to my friend Tony, who suggested the Shopaholica category to me, she enjoys your devotion and adulation. She loves being adored. She is a Player of sorts. It's not that she is unfaithful. She never gives you the impression that you are the only one, so she is not exactly cheating. It is just that she accepts your affection with no promise of ever returning it, because you are not good enough. She is still looking.

Just One More

To a certain type of Shopaholica, you are just one more in a long string of conquests. To underscore this point, she will tell you about other men she has had. While you are lying exhausted in each other's arms after making love, she will tell you about the characteristics and quirks of other men's private parts she has experienced: One man was a lefty, another was a righty; one had a growth shaped like Rhode Island on the tip, one was hung like a mosquito, one was tattooed to look like a scaly green snake decorated with gold piercings, and the one before you was "packing like a porn star." It is more than you want to know and kills the intimacy of the moment with your dream girl. Then, to make matters even less comfortable, she tells you how her ideal looks and it doesn't resemble yours in the least.

My Mamma Told Me . . . .

Some Shopaholicas cannot make up their minds, ever. They take Smokey Robinson's song, "My mamma told me, you better shop around," literally and perpetually. They are like that about everything in their lives, so why not men too? They will shop all day for a skirt and not find the exact one they want, go home exhausted and start again another day, never satisfied. If you are the man of the moment, you will distinctly feel this slight dissatisfaction with you. You are the skirt that she has settled for at the moment because she has to wear something. But she might exchange you the next day for another one.

MAMMA SHOPAHOLICA

Illusion versus Reality
Shopaholica is always looking for the ideal. The current reality is not good enough for her. She keeps looking for something better. That can be a problem when she has children. She wants to have the ideal baby, a plump, dimpled charmer whose twinkling eyes never shed a tear and who gurgles and coos happily all through the day, sleeping peacefully all night long. When the real baby comes along and does not meet these criteria, she becomes disappointed. She looks at pictures in magazines and at other people's babies and thinks they are much prettier than hers are. This wrinkled, unhappy, demanding food processor in diapers is nothing like the picture of the baby on the baby food jar!

Children do pick up on these attitudes in their early years and can spend a lifetime getting Mommy to love and accept them for who and what they are, knowing that they can never be like the air-brushed wonders their mother really wants.

Perfection Fixation
As the children get older they are quite aware that Mom is disappointed in them. Their grades are never good enough,

they are not as athletic as Pat's kids down the street are, they are not as good-looking as those catalogue models, they are not, they are not, they are not. Their self-esteem plummets and makes them potential victims for future Shopaholicas, whose principal prey consists of men with low self-esteem. Shopaholica Mom compares her children with others because "over there" is naturally better than "over here." Someone else always has it better in this perfectionist's world.

Settling

Shopaholica has difficulty settling down because she cannot make up her mind. Therefore there is less danger that she will reproduce herself than the other Dirty Seven Sisters. But when Shopaholica does settle down, it is because she has "settled for" someone. She knows she should have married Larry but settled for Harry. So, how could her kids turn out well? What could she expect? She might even think out loud during moments of anger: "No wonder you're the way you are, you don't stand a chance with a father like yours. I should have married Larry. He was so good-looking and he made good money too, not like your dad!" Don't inflict this kind of mother on an innocent child by waiting around for her until she marries you in desperation. No one else will have her, so she will settle for you.

SHOPAHOLICA EXAMPLES

It Ain't You, Babe!

Anthony had known Rita since childhood and had a huge crush on her since the eighth grade, when he sat next to her in Social Studies. They listened to Bob Dylan songs together through High School. Their favorite song was "It Ain't Me, Babe." Anthony didn't realize at the time how prophetic those words would be.

He took her to the prom, but it hadn't been a straightforward thing. She really wanted to go with Mel, but Mel didn't ask her, so after turning Anthony down when he first asked her, she phoned him and said she had changed her mind and wanted to go with him after all.

Anthony put a lot of thought into the evening and tried to make it as special as he could for her. He bought the costliest orchids, rented a limo, and planned an after-prom surprise. He noticed that she was distracted. When they danced together, he could feel her attention was not with him. She was looking around the room to spot Mel with his date. When they sat down, he could also see her scanning the room. She barely talked to him. He felt he had gone to a lot of trouble so she should not be treating him like second best.

Nevertheless, he was so much in love with her, he continued to hang on for years after they had graduated. He was her backup date when any of the others fell through, or if no one else asked her out for a Saturday night. He honestly felt that she would finally see that he was the one for her because they got along so well. But reality dawned at her and Mel's wedding. When the band was playing their old favorite she walked over, ethereal in her white satin gown, and asked Anthony to dance.

"Thanks, Anthony, for sticking by me all the years while Mel was ignoring me," she said as she looked into his eyes. "You are a great man and I know you will make someone very happy one day." She then started singing along with the band's schmaltzy version of Bob Dylan's, "It ain't me babe, no, no, no, it ain't me, babe, it ain't me you're lookin' for, babe!"

Born to Shop

Zach saw Celine writhing rhythmically under the disco ball at the club. The strobe lights gave her an otherworldly aspect that more than intrigued him. He had to get to know this woman! He asked her to go out with him after a few dances. She told him she was already living with a man named Joel but they weren't getting along, so if he didn't mind that she was already with someone, she would be glad to go out with him. Zach admired the fact that she was so straightforward with him about her live-in situation and wasn't trying to play him by lying.

They had some great times going out together. She despised her current boyfriend and told Zach all kinds of things about him, his temper, his hygiene, and his infidelity to her. Zach listened with sympathy. What a jerk this man was! He told her she could move in with him and forget Joel. Why was she staying with him if she was so unhappy? "No, I couldn't do that," Celine said, "I haven't figured out if you're the one for me yet. I can't hop from the frying pan into the fire."

Zach thought this was strange. It was irrational that she'd rather live with Joel, who had all kinds of behavior problems, and not with him, who was bending over backwards to make her happy. He figured that the word "yet" meant that he had to earn the right to her presence by repeatedly showing her that he wasn't like Joel. Or, maybe it meant that she had been traumatized by her current living situation and couldn't just jump into another one, no matter how nice he was.

One night, as he was talking with his friend Alex over a beer, he mentioned his problem about Celine. "That's funny," Alex said, "I'm seeing a girl named Celine too! That's not a common name. Tell me more about her."

Anthony told him where they met. Alex turned red as the possibility dawned, "I met her at that club too. She was a thing of enchantment, gyrating under the lights like a wet dream from another realm." They compared other things, down to the information about Joel. It all was the same, every line, even down to how he chewed tobacco and ate breakfast at the same time. They described in unison how the oatmeal and tobacco juice drooled out of the corners of his mouth.

"Unbelievable!" Anthony howled, "How many more of us are there in Miss Celine s little shopping cart?" They informally staked out her place like makeshift detectives, sitting in a car across the street. They spotted two men walking out of her place with her at different times, hugging, kissing, arms intertwined. Anthony was stunned at this prodigious example of Shopaholica's behavior. Somehow he thought that being a player was reserved for members of his own sex and the beautiful girls he knew couldn't be like that. Girls were nicer than men, weren't they? Especially such meltingly pretty ones, right?

As if!

Shellie tolerated Al because he was obviously in love with her. But she really did not want to be seen with him because he needed to lose weight and he was not her type. Nevertheless, he was good for a loan and a booty call and so she kept him in a holding pattern for five years.

Shellie was known as a "hottie" and even Al knew he was known as a "geek," "dweeb," or "nerd ." Shellie never told him this but he knew it was going on in her mind. Nevertheless, she could be so nice with him. They were great in bed together. She did not seem to mind his extra 75 pounds when she clamped her legs around his back or rode him like a rodeo bull rider. No, they could go at it for hours. Sometimes she went out with one of the good-looking men on a fancy date and later called Al. "Hi, this is Shellie, come over, I just got home from a date."

One night they were lying, tangled in damp sheets after a marathon session and Al whispered, "I love you. Stay with me. Let's be together." Her beauty stunned him as her lips curled into a smile. It quickly turned into the twisted smile of derision. "As if! You don't really think I feel anything for you do you? I've been stringing you along for years and you were too stupid not to see through it, Al! Get real! I wouldn't be caught dead in public with a man like you. Look, it's been fun, but it's time to move on. You should be happy that I'm being so honest with you!" She began to stroke his head.

Al felt like he had just been plunged into a bucket of ice. My God, did she have to be so mean about it? He wondered why he loved her so intensely. Didn't she even have any feeling for him at all? No, she didn't. He was no more to her than a seasonal pet, in the way that some people adopt a cat for the summer at the shore. Now it was time for her to ditch him on the side of the road or drop him at the pound. Didn't she tell him once, "I could really love you, Al, I could really love you?" That's why he stuck around all those years. He thought he could do enough nice things for her to make her see that she really cared for him and wanted him to be hers alone.

Free Love

Andreas asked out an attractive woman he met in a bookstore. No matter where they went that evening: the movie, the restaurant, the club, it seemed she knew every man that walked through the door. She called each one over, gave each a big hug and kiss, and talked with him flirtatiously for several minutes. When she wasn't greeting the endless stream of men, she was scanning the room, checking out all the other men in the place. When Andreas finally could not take anymore, he suggested they call it a night. She then asked him if he could drop her off at a friend's house. Reluctantly, he agreed. This "friend" turned out to be a man, whom she gave a very passionate kiss when he opened the door to his house. Then she turned and waved to Andreas as he sat totally humiliated in his car, and said, "It was fun, let's do it again sometime. Call me?"

"Right!" he sneered. "I had a great time. I love being used. Let's not do it again!"

Ask Him out for Me!

This story, in Jared's own words, illustrates a type of Shopaholica attitude all men would do best to avoid: "Last year I liked this girl Emma from my school. She knew I had a really big crush on her. But we were pretty good friends . . . until I asked her out. She rejected me and said I wasn't her type.

"Then she started asking advice about this other man, Wallace, and to make a long story short, I ended up asking him out for her. He turned her down, but I was there to console her. After about a month I asked her out again, still no luck.

"The very next day she tells my friend that she likes this freshman, Carl, who is the biggest JACKASS I know. Again she comes to me for advice. Again I end up asking him out for her too. He too rejects her. Then she whines to me about not being able to get a decent man!"

CELEBRITY SHOPAHOLICAS

Julia

Some people might point out that the beautiful Julia Roberts appears to be a Shopaholica. They question why she needs to fall in love with and declare her undying devotion to every leading man in her movies. Her love affairs have the longevity of a mayfly's brief life span. Where is the depth or meaning to the word love when it changes with such frequency? The rush of novelty, the promise of romance in a never-never land of movie sets and fantasy cannot stand up to the glare of everyday reality and it all falls apart. Oh well, on to the next one! More will follow to become fodder for stand up comics, late-night talk shows, and the tabloids.

There is, of course, an immutable law of celebrity: The more nauseatingly and insistently two stars proclaim their togetherness, the closer they are to coming apart. Witness Pamela Anderson and Tommy Lee, Jennifer Lopez and Puffy, or Angelina Jolie and Billy Bob Thornton. Meanwhile, celebrity couples that evidence staying power, like Tom Hanks and Rita Wilson, Paul Newman and Joanne Woodward, tend not to conduct interviews with their legs coiled around each other's heads while sucking the life out of each other's faces. These hyper-displays are no substitute for what really matters in a love relationship: responsibility, fidelity, and mental stability -- all qualities lacking in Shopaholica.

Cher
On her 40th birthday Cher saw the 22-year-old bagel-vending hunk Rob Camilletti for the first time and said, "Have him washed and brought to my tent. A girl can wait for the right man to come along," she explained, "but in the meantime that still doesn't mean she can't have a wonderful time with all the wrong ones." That approximates the attitude of Shopaholica. It can be fun while it lasts. Just do not get your heart broken in the process by thinking it's real. Did Rob Camilletti think he was going to settle down with Cher for ever and ever? Probably not, but he was happy to have the experience of being with her for the moment.

Prevention: Self-esteem

Battery Not Included

Show business apart, men who stay with Shopaholicas are like the battered spouses of abusive men. It is puzzling to try to understand why the battered wife keeps returning to her husband after he brutalizes her. It is equally as puzzling to understand why men hang around Shopaholicas, thinking that one day they will be the chosen ones. Though a Shopaholica will not bruise and beat you, your ego will be battered enough as you realize that you are not and never will be "The One." It is a self-esteem issue with all mentally or physically battered people who continue to tolerate their second-class citizenship.

Easier said . . .

Self-esteem is a large topic and the subject of scores of books. Many things happen to a man to cause him to have low self-esteem, usually when he is too young to defend himself against his detractors. Other children and the adults around him teach him that somehow he is not as smart, good-looking, skilled, or popular as others are. Building up self-esteem after years of believing that you are not good enough takes time and awareness. It is not as easy as telling someone, "Have more self-esteem, don't waste your life waiting for a woman who is just playing with you because she has nothing better to do." Whatever your esteem issues are, the best I can do is tell you to avoid Shopaholicas. They are not going to settle down with you because they do not settle down. However, if your self-esteem problems drive you to seek her out, you will play out the same drama over and over again with no curtain call. You will sit like a hopeful puppy, waiting for Miss Shopaholica to throw you a steak, when all you will get is a well-gnawed bone.

Eye, Eye Sir!
One way to detect if you are with a Shopaholica is how she looks at you. Are her eyes all over the room or does she look into your face and concentrate on you while you are talking? Do you see her flirting with the man across the room or is she really with you while at a party or when you are eating out? Does she tell you she loves your looks or is she constantly showing you magazine pictures of how she wishes you looked, while she is drooling all over the page? Do her eyes tell you that she is happy to be with you and you alone? If you answer yes to the first part of each of these questions and no to the second, your lady is not a Shopaholica.

History Lesson
Listen to her stories of past relationships. Was she able to hold onto a relationship for any length of time? Why did the relationships not work out? Shopaholicas usually blame the man for not being good enough and they are the ones who initiate the break-up. In this age of serial monogamy, it is not a horrible thing for a woman to have had a number of relationships over the course of a lifetime. But if all of them had the importance and weight of a Pit Stop on the way to the finish line, start looking for the Exit sign. You will be just one more stop along the way too, so you might as well shorten the time you will waste on this win-lose relationship (she wins, you lose).

THE WEDDING BELLE

WEDDING BELLE BLUES

Picture Book Marriage

The Wedding Belle is obsessed with marriage. She will not rest until she fulfills her dreams. Beware if you have become the target of her nuptial fantasies or breeding plans. She will usually bring up marriage on the first date and every subsequent date as long as you keep asking her out. She wants that picture book marriage and will not let you forget it.

Ceremoniac and Baby Crazo

Wedding Belles come in two varieties:

- Ceremoniac
- Baby Crazo

They both live in a fantasy world of bridal and house-keeping magazines, books on perfect settings for marriages, idealized babies, and art-directed wedded bliss. You are like the male doll on the top of the wedding cake in a fairy tale that stops short after the marriage ceremony is over. You are Ken in Barbie's perfect Dream House but there is no "happily ever after" for you in this plastic kingdom.

Ceremonymania

The Ceremoniac Wedding Belle wants to get married at any cost. Marriage itself is more important than whom she is marrying. Ever since she was a little girl, she has had one goal in life: To get married and have a huge, fairy tale wedding. She devotes all her thought to the wedding and very little to the relationship. It is all about the gloss, the glitz, the ornate ritual that symbolizes the union of two beings in love, but stops short at the ceremony. She is playing with sets and decor, not the actuality of two beings sharing love in a lifetime union.

First Date Warning Bells

Ceremoniac cuts to the chase early on the first date. She is already naming your kids in her head as you start on the salad. As you nibble on bread, she is pairing her first name with your last name in pencil on the place mat. You are halfway through the main course when she brings up the wedding itself, "What kind of ceremony do you prefer, large and splashy or small and intimate? I'm torn between the two. All my friends are getting married lately! It's like that old expression, 'Always a bridesmaid, never a bride!' You should have seen my friend Adriana's wedding! She had four stretch limos and three restored carriages lined in blue satin, drawn by teams of six horses each, on loan from the Budweiser estate! The bridesmaids were wearing lavender-dyed vintage lace over mauve watered silk, all hand-sewn by a mother and daughter team flown in from Italy just for the occasion. Oh, and her dress, My God, I have a picture of it in my purse. Let me get it out."

Wedding Cake Dress

"No rush," you want to say, while she is unfolding a worn and creased full-length picture of what looks like a woman wearing a wedding cake. It is a mountain of ornate frosting, studded with seed pearls. She goes on about the details of the headdress, the train, and the flowers, while your mind drifts. Your car needs a tune-up. You'll take care of it tomorrow. Her voice fades into the background as you tune out. Why does this woman think that you are automatically fascinated by the overpriced details of her friend's matrimonial ceremony? Her blindness to your needs in favor of fulfilling hers makes her a particularly irritating member of the Dirty Seven sisterhood.

It Gets Worse

If this conversation bores you, get out now. Wedding Belles do not get more interesting after marriage. Since the bulk of their conversation consists of the wedding plans before marriage, they do not have much to talk about after it is over. Some Wedding Belles completely let themselves go once they are married. The wedding is the climax of their lives. The rest is anticlimax, especially regarding sex. Their interpretation of living "happily ever after" is to go unwashed, uncombed, and ungroomed, being slovenly housekeepers, and not bothering to please their prey any more in bed.

Wifie-poo

Other ceremoniacs show themselves to be picture-perfect "wifies" and mothers. You, however, are nothing more than a means to an end: The vehicle carrying her from Point A: Non-marriage, to Point B: Marriage. Once you have done your job, get out of the way. They have trapped a husband and accomplished their life's goal. They stop trying to be nice to you any more. Whether they do a Cinderella in reverse into slovenliness, or keep a spotless house and act like Martha Stewart's twin sister, Wedding Belles are the mistresses of the bait and switch tactics among the Dirty Seven Sisters. They act one way before marriage and pull a switcheroo on you afterwards.

BABY CRAZO

Sperm Donor
The Baby Crazo Wedding Belle is motivated to be with you because she wants children badly. She is mainly interested in you as a sperm donor. She desires the trappings of a marriage and a family, but you as a person are not a top priority on her scale of interests. She does, however require you to have certain characteristics to be an ideal father. She might require certain talents and appearance factors, but after that you can bow out as being meaningful in her life. Once you have spawned, like the salmon that fights his way upstream each mating season and dies, you have served your function. You get the feeling that you are just a meal ticket to enable the little picture book family she has always wanted.

Ooops!
She ropes you into parenthood, sometimes by not using birth control when she says she has been using it. "I need to tell you something. I'm pregnant. I should have told you I wasn't using birth control. I lied because I wanted a baby so

badly." You are not amused. You are not ready to support a child yet and now you must get a second job to take care of the situation.

Who Are You?
Then she stays home and tends the kiddies while you go out to support her. When you come home, she does not look happy to see you. She has a list of complaints and demands and household chores. Her affection is reserved for the baby, highlighting her indifference to you. When you walk through the door after a day working for her, she gives you a look expressing: "Who are you?" You will never find warmth or happiness with this type of Wedding Belle. You will only have the appearance of marriage with none of the love or affinity behind it.

Aging Eggs
Here is another scenario: You are out on a light-hearted date with a great-looking girl. As you look out over the skyline together she turns to you and asks, "Do you want to have kids one day?" Already, the mood is potentially destroyed. You do not know where she is going with this and it could be fraught with landmines. If you say "No," you will have to explain yourself. You might want them one day, but not right away, so you say, "Yes." Then you realize you should have said "No." The entire evening turns into her monologue on children and how much she wants to have them. She tells you that her biological clock is ticking away. She's getting older, and her limited store of eggs is dwindling. Her eggs are aging too and also decreasing in number. She needs to have babies now before her eggs shrivel up and die, like raisins in the shrunken husk that was

once her uterus.

Romance Killer

The romance of the moment is completely squashed as you picture her innards. You can picture her fleshly plumbing rusting away. The romance is further strangled by images of Lamaze classes, parenting magazines, and standing in long lines at toy outlets. You can see this beauty turning into one of those mommies whose lives are consumed with babies. She will call you "Daddy" and use baby talk most of the day. If you ask her how she spent her day, be prepared to hear some major baby talk: "We had to go to the dockie-wockie because Tommie-Wommie was sickie-wickie. We gots to take those pinky-winky pillzie-willzies and now sweetie-weetie is cranky-wanky. We've gots to take our nappie-wappie, don't we honey-bunny? I told him if he's good, we'll all go to the Kiddie Kastle on Saturday, OK Daddy?"

Kiddie Kastle

You are thinking that it would be great to have a real conversation with a love partner, but paying attention to you is way down on Baby Crazo's activity list today and every day. You can imagine the hours of baby talk and dull silence you will endure as you wheel a stroller from ride to ride at the Kiddie Kastle. The most interesting discussion you will have will be a price comparison of disposable diapers. And do not think you will be compensated by a great sex life with her either. She is finished with you as a sex partner, unless it is time for her to have another baby. Then she deploys the troops and you better be ready for action when the time is right.

I'm Ready Now!

If Baby Crazo has her mind set on another baby, she will make sure that your starvation diet turns into a bonanza of mechanical sex. She makes you quite aware of your function as a reproductive machine. She will lie on the bed, legs apart, "Come on, hurry it up. I'm going through my most fertile time of the month, ovulation, now and I don't want to waste any time. Besides, Tommie's asleep so we have about five minutes. What are you waiting for?" She removes her dingy panties that hang in folds around her butt. They fall to the floor in a tattle-tale gray heap.

Somehow you do not feel like "doing it" but you strip obediently. She stares at the ceiling while you pump away at her, trying to get enough friction to maintain an erection and be able to ejaculate within the allotted time. You begin to fantasize about a warm, loving woman who appreciates you, who shows affection and respect. You imagine a companion and friend who is playful and sensuous. You finally manage to expel your seed into Baby Crazo's pelvic cavity. You hope one of your little tadpoles will puncture her egg and burrow its microscopic head within, so you can get some rest. Sex on demand sounds good in theory but is a problem in practice if you are doing it with a drill sergeant in granny-panties.

WEDDING BELLE MAMAS

Super Moms

Wedding Belles often become Super Moms. They schedule every minute of their children's day with precision. The storybook family must have children who go to karate, soccer, music practice, beauty pageants, scouts, dance, gymnastics, etc. She belongs to every organization, PTA, Garden Club, Welcome Wagon, Junior League, etc. Not that these activities and clubs are bad in themselves; the quantity of activities she volunteers leave scanty time for you. By the time she finishes her roster of activities she has little interest in sex or love at the end of her exhausting day. Society might applaud her but you will not as you realize how lonely you are with this program director.

Neglect
Another type of Wedding Belle Mom is the one who has the children and then neglects them as much as she neglects herself. The ceremony is over and the real world is of no interest to her. You will be left with much of the childcare. She seems to have no maternal instinct or mothering skills. She might lie around on the couch reading romance novels. She is lost in the make-believe wedding of the bodice ripper heroine embracing Fabio on the pink and gold cover, while the kids run around in soaked diapers with dirty faces, hungry until you get home to feed them. You had managed to impregnate her but you wonder how you did it. Nowadays she is indifferent to your sexual advances and lies there as unappetizing as 3-week-old mackerel.

Typically, you come home from work and find you have to go out again to get some food for dinner. Then you have to cook it. How can you expect her to help out? She has a headache and has to lie on the couch and read and sleep. Besides, Angelique is just about to elope, against her wealthy daddy's wishes, with Fabio! So you feed the kids, bathe them, and put them to bed. Then you go back to the kitchen to clean up the dishes. You pass her shapeless mass as she sprawls on the couch. "Am I having fun yet?"

Baby Crazoid

As a mother, Baby Crazo Wedding Belle is the opposite of the Neglectful variety. She can be overprotective and obsessed with the safety of her kiddies. As noted in the section on the Kiddie Kastle, her conversation centers on everything the baby said, did, didn't say, and didn't do. She has no life of her own and no original thoughts. She is afraid to let her babies play with other babies for they might get hurt or catch something. She wraps them in so many sweaters and scarves on winter days, they look like mummies and can hardly move if they do manage to play with others.

If you ask her about world events or about ideas of any kind, she will go blank because her mental ruts are grooved in only one direction: The baby. She will tell you a long story about Little Georgie's constipation that rivals *The Odyssey* in length and complexity. Her every thought being focused on the kids leaves no room for you. This is actually a relief, as noted before, because her baby talk is not sexy. Through it, she expresses herself on the level of a 2-year-old. Baby talk 24/7 is a turn-off in bed if you want sex with a full-fledged woman who has passion and feelings for you as a man.

WEDDING BELLE EXAMPLES

The Personal Ad-venture

Francine sounded good to Malcolm when he read her personal ad: "30s, buxom, Pam Anderson look-alike, professional, blond, attractive." He replied and invited her out to dinner. She turned out to be a 39 year-old, disheveled 400-pound divorced secretary with four kids. When she finally shoehorned herself into a booth, her basketball-sized bosoms were displayed prominently on the table, catching food droppings as she slurped the contents of her plate. She was talking so much and so fast about herself and her plans she didn't even hear Malcolm when he suggested she looked uncomfortable and they could wait for seating at a table. By the end of the meal, she said "You're kinda cute! Would you be interested in a long-term relationship, starting tonight?"

Malcolm was abashed. Their conversation did not reveal the sort of person he was and he in no way disclosed his suitability for a long-term relationship, nor did he give the slightest impression he'd be interested in seeing her again. He wanted to be candid. He wanted to say something about legal penalties for untruthful advertising. He lied. He told her he had arrangements to meet with a number of other ad dates. Then she got angry, "Are you saying I'm not good enough for you? No. I thought you were interested in long-term. I am. If I wanted this rejection shit I could have stayed married."

"Perhaps she should've," thought Malcolm. She called him later to say that she was sorry and wanted to go out with him again. She told him she was sure he would be interested in marriage with her the next time he saw her.

Now and Then

Ed came home to see Suki on the couch in what looked like the same position he left her that morning when he went off to work. He didn't understand what had happened to her. The beautiful bride of a year ago, with her shiny, clean hair was this lumpen mass, watching daytime television and not doing much else. Pictures of their stupendous wedding were all over the house in huge, leather and gold frames. Sparkling eyes punctuated the frozen smile on her face as she lived the dream of her lifetime. But now the dream was over and reality had set in.

Overflowing garbage cans, dirty floors, dusty furniture, and clutter were all so overwhelming to Suki. All she could do was sit on the couch and wait for Ed to come home to take care of it. She had done her job and married him. She had not thought beyond that and now it was up to him to take care of the rest. Life was too disappointing to her. It wasn't endless wedding cake and photographers and flowers and organ music. It was plain old reality and she was plain old Suki, sitting on the couch in her funky sweats.

Rubber Glove Treatment

Five minutes after we were introduced at a party, Christine disappeared and returned with a large, lace-decorated photo album bursting with wedding pictures. We just met, yet already she wanted to show me this ornate validation of herself. Fifteen minutes later, my eyes involuntarily rolled up in my head and stayed there as she got to the obligatory shot of the bride and groom stuffing each other's mouths with wedding cake. The yawn that was emerging from my mouth almost dislocated my jaw. I excused myself and drifted into another room. She found me an hour later. By this time a few glasses of Chablis had loosened her tongue even more.

She wanted to confide in me about her marriage. She told me she was very disappointed in her husband. She wanted everything to be perfect but he wanted to have sex at least once a week and she wasn't interested in it at all. Why were men such animals? He was ruining the awesome beauty of her wedding memories with his demands. Disgusted as she was, she told him he could have it once every two weeks. She said she used a rubber glove on him at arms' length. Did he really expect her to touch it with her bare hands?

I asked her if she had been intimate with him before marriage. She said, "No, I told him I was saving it for marriage. But when the time came for me to give it up, I just really didn't want to. Our honeymoon was a disaster because I refused to have sex with him. He was angry with me about it. He said I got him to marry me under false pretenses and that I didn't hold up my end of the bargain.

"I got mad at him because I felt all he wanted was sex and just married me to get it. I told him I really hated sex but just wanted the wedding, basically. I had been dreaming about it since I was five years old, when my whole world was my *Dream Wedding Barbie* doll. I had all three of the "Wedding Barbies," the *Sophisticated Wedding Barbie* and the *Millenium Wedding Barbie* too! So, anyway, we agreed on the weekly rubber glove rubdown as a compromise and now at least he leaves me alone about it. It only takes a few minutes and I don't look anyway."

"So I guess you don't want to have kids?" I asked. "That's an ingenious means of birth control!" She said, "Oh yeah, I really want to have kids to complete the picture but not right now. When the time comes, I'll let him, you know, have, like, sex with me. Eeuuww! Right now we've got to work to afford that nursery set I saw in *Architectural Digest.* I can't get it out of my mind! I guess I'll have to get it over with to have a baby. A baby would look so cute in the fantastic restored antique crib that's my latest obsession!"

CELEBRITY WEDDING BELLES

I Need "A Child"

Often, a celebrity will take a look around her life and find that she has acquired all the symbols of success, but she does not have a family. She has sacrificed personal relationships to a work schedule that includes traveling, appearances, early-morning shoots, and late-night parties. "What good is all of this? It doesn't make me happy after all. I need a child!" So she introduces an offspring into this world, yet within a guaranteed two years after the fantastic event, "separation" and then "divorce" become new words in the child's vocabulary. The list of celebrity marriages that have collapsed, leaving kids in the middle of a custody battle, runs like an A-Z of broken relationships. It is all part of the show.

Sperm Banks

"A Child" becomes another personal adornment for publicity. The father is not a necessary accompaniment to the system, since female celebrities can afford to rear a child on their own or with a female partner. Therefore, some female celebrities use men as sperm banks. However, these ladies are not the best examples of Baby Crazos, who usually parasitize men for the child's material support. Gay celebrity mothers, such as Rosie O'Donnell and Melissa Etheridge, single mothers like Sandra Bernhardt and Elizabeth Hurley, and formerly single mothers like Madonna, have displayed their beliefs that the presence of a male was totally unnecessary for the growth and development of a child.

Kate

Harper's Bazaar's best dressed 2001 list featured the 20 most stylish women on the planet, each with a statement on the item they wish they could wear but for some reason cannot. The supermodel Kate Moss said, "A wedding dress." Kate often wore wedding dresses on the catwalk but now she wanted one in real life. She claimed elsewhere that she was trying for a baby with Jefferson Hack, her boyfriend of sixth months. She has enough money to keep herself in Gucci forever, and yet all she wants is the only dress that money alone cannot buy. The drugs, the booze, the cigarettes are not working anymore. The biggest high now is the latest fashion craze: The celebrity wedding and then a child, or maybe a child first and then the celebrity wedding.

Celebrity Ceremoniacs

Celebrity wedding extravaganzas like Liz Taylor's marriage to Larry Fortensky, Richard Burton, and others seem like so much whipped cream on top of a gooey sundae. The fanfare, the publicity, the expense, all to end a few years later in the Celebrity Divorce, and more publicity. These weddings are like giant movie sets or Busby Berkley musicals, with helicopters and paparazzi swirling around the outskirts and the whole world watching the spectacle on TV.

Brooke

Brooke Shields and Andre Agassi had a huge wedding but after the wedding saw each other infrequently. She lived in LA - where her show was filmed - spending just one week a month visiting Agassi, whose work kept him in Las Vegas and on the world tennis circuit. Did she honestly think this union would work? She admitted that her dreams exceeded her reality. She said their first 12 months of marriage had been "the hardest of my life." She longed to have a baby, saying: "I thought we would be parents by now. But with Andre away so much it's difficult." She wanted to have a baby so badly she was blind to the circumstances. You have to be there to get pregnant. Wedding Belles want marriage at all costs, including incompatibility. In the divorce papers, Andre Agassi said the pair had drifted so far apart they had nothing in common. Andre Agassi's lawyer Earl Monsey said in an 11-page document: "Andre Agassi and Brooke Shields are incompatible in their tastes, natures, views, likes and dislikes, which have become widely separate and divergent so that the parties now are totally incompatible."

Marilyn

Marilyn Monroe and Joe DiMaggio had a hugely publicized ceremony but the marriage, like her others, did not last. Why did men leave this beauty? Though a ravishing sex symbol on screen, in life she was a combination Needee Nellie and Wedding Belle. She was desperate to be loved, could not be reassured enough by one man, and needed to prove that she was loved by masses of men. Once married, she disappointed the husbands who married the dream, which continues to enchant an entire population to this day. Thoughtless and self-absorbed, addicted to pills and booze, she could barely get herself up in the morning. Her work habits were slovenly; she was notoriously late and unprepared. She was an internal wreck who needed help, not adoration, which she never trusted anyway when the makeup wore off.

PREVENTION: FAIR WARNING

Early Detection

Fortunately for you, the Wedding Belle is easy to detect early on. She tips you off through her incessant talk about marriage, weddings, and children, usually on the first date. She might be able to keep it under wraps until the third date through effortful self-restraint. But after that, her robotic fixation on getting hitched will display itself in myriad ways. She will ooh and ahh over every baby that crosses your path when you are out together, if she is a Baby Crazo. The Ceremoniac blabs on about her friends' weddings or her own imagined dream wedding. Both types of Wedding Belles betray their agendas too soon. Their desperation to get married or have a child comes through in every sentence they utter.

Warning Signals

Like Needee Nellies, Wedding Belles are easy to spot by their conversational cues. But, while Needee Nellie needs endless love and assurance, these Dirty Seven Sisters can easily do without them. They are only interested in the symbol of mutual love, not the reality. The symbol, the wedding, is their all-in-all. The reality, the actual marriage of two people who love and support each other as they build a life together, is not as important to them. Don't expect them to understand that marriage means a commitment to hold up their end of the relationship, to love and understand you, and to be a companion. Their minds are like filing cabinets containing one folder labeled "The Wedding."

Listen to the warning bells when a Wedding Belle talks about getting married on the first or second date, or even after a few weeks or a month. If you continue with her after this, notice how often she brings up marriage and children. She may have no other topic of conversation, because she has not thought about anything else for years. She does not live in the present moment, she is living for the future. Once the future arrives and the wedding is over, so will be your happiness.

THE MOM

YOU'RE JUST ONE OF THE KIDS

Mommy Dearest

The Mom is the lady who always knows better and more than you do. She is always right. You are always wrong. She is the Mrs. Right in the joke: "I married Mrs. Right. I just didn't know her first name was Always." You are the incompetent bozo who needs to be set straight by her, since she knows it all and you can never hope to ascend to her pinnacle of knowledge and common sense.

Yes, Mom!

You are just one of the kids in her eyes. You are not an adult with logical, discretionary intelligence, especially after marriage. She does not trust you to do anything correctly so she does it all. She watches you when you volunteer to wash dishes. Instead of being thankful that you are doing something to help out, she grabs the soap and sponge out of your hands and says, "Here, let me do this! Can't you do anything right? I swear, you're just like one of the kids! Do I have to be everyone's Mom? Now watch me! Who said you could leave? I said, 'Stand here and watch me!'" She cracks the whip and expects you to jump.

Laying Carpet

The Mom regards sex as a reward, like candy, to give you after you have been a good boy. When you are married to her, she has a long to-do list for you every weekend. Like Roy's wife Alice, she says things like, "You won't get laid unless the carpet gets laid." Then she watches over you to make sure you are doing everything properly, clucking loudly when she thinks you are making a mistake and ultimately snatching your tools away from you to do it herself. You figure you are not going to get any loving tonight, again! But that is all right too, in a way. She can be just as dictatorial in bed as she is out of it. Or else she shows obvious boredom with the ordeal, because, once again, you never do anything right.

Sergeant Mom

Let us say you get lucky and have done all your chores like a good little boy. The Mom will have sex with you now, and it better be good! She gives you instructions like a marine sergeant, "Lower, higher, harder, slower, faster, lighter, over to the right, now the left. Here, let me do it myself. I can do it better than you can!" When it's over she will debrief you on where you went wrong and what you did right. Since she is the only one allowed to be right in this relationship, you always come up being (guess what?) wrong again! Your lovemaking sessions become grueling guessing games about whether you are doing it right or not. You cannot tell, because she gives no indication of enjoyment.

Granny Panties

She wears underwear you remember seeing on your grandmother's clothesline: Billowy white pantaloons that she pulls up to just under her breasts. Her mammary glands are encased in what appears to be a big, utilitarian nursing bra. She acts like she does not want to be an object of desire and kills the male libido with her no-fun approach to life and the bedroom. My friend Ari described his wife

Hilda as, "A scolding nag in a baggy Hawaiian muumuu. She's more like my mother than my own mother and that doesn't work for me in bed." Her bedroom dialog is something like this:

> **Hilda** (Sitting in bed with a book, wearing a large, flowered muumuu, her hair wrapped around heated rollers): Do you want to have sex? Because, I'm really exhausted from driving the kids around all day. And besides you've got to get up early tomorrow to Rototill the garden and then take the tiller back over to Nelson's before 7:00.

> **Ari** (Lying beside her in bed smiling): How about just cuddling with me for a while?

> **Hilda** (wrinkling her face as if she just swallowed a tarantula and its furry limbs were caught in her throat): No, the kids are still awake, and besides, I know you, cuddling leads to sex and I'm just too tired! After taking care of the kids all day, the last thing on my mind is sex. It's more of a chore than anything else to me. Besides, you didn't polish the brass fixtures in the bathroom the way I told you to today or fix the screws you put in the wrong way! When are you going to stop being such a baby and do things right? Grow up! Until you put those screws in right, you won't be getting any screwing from me!

The Mom as Mom

Tsk, tsk!

As stated, the kids come first with The Mom. They know it and she reminds them of it every day. One of her behaviors is to instill guilt in them about how much she has sacrificed for them because they are the center of her world. Therein lies the paradox. She treats you like one of the kids, but you are definitely not the center of her life in the way they are. She demonstrates this to you in many ways. She might run behind you with a broom, sweeping up the mess you brought in with you or otherwise remind you that you are making things dirty or sloppy. She inspects your hair and nails and dictates what you wear. Then she puts you down in front of your children and scolds you like a naughty boy for wearing those old jeans again. She thought she had thrown them out! Who gave you permission to get them out of the garbage? Her disrespect for you does not encourage your children to respect you either.

You Naughty Boy!

You might have gotten used to her put-downs in public and in front of your friends and family, but it rankles when she undermines your children's regard for you. She does not trust one decision you make and lets them know about it. And furthermore, you don't make enough money! She complains about that too as she lists all the things that are wrong with you as a man, father, husband, and human being. You have become one big disappointment to her. If you only would listen and do everything she says, you might stand a chance, but just maybe. You are her naughty little boy and she is just about to give up on you! Her motto is Judge Judy's famous: "I am smarter on my worst day, than you on your best day."

Kids Rule

Since the kids are the purpose and substance of The Mom's life, it does not seem fair that she treats you like a child without any of the benefits of being one in her world. You are more like the unwanted leftover in a dysfunctional foster home than one of her own. Your own children see you as an ineffectual add-on that just happens to bring home the money to support the household. They tolerate you the way she does, but you do not have a real vote in household matters. You are the disappointingly silly imbecilic, lovable old Dad. If The Mom weren't around, the ship would sink into the ocean of ineffectuality. She loves control and in this navy there is only one captain: The Mom.

Stage and Pageant Moms

A different type of Mom lives through her children, to an unhealthy degree, while you stand by and watch the parade. This is the Stage and Pageant Mom. She takes her kids appearance on stage much too seriously, as if the child is her stand-in on the stage of life itself. Dressing a child up like a miniature sex kitten to replace the action she is missing from her own life can affect her child badly. The pressure to win and not disappoint Mom is intense for this child. She has to live with Mom the next day and ever after if the judges do not give her an award. Hair and makeup sessions and endless practice to prime her to be the prettiest little girl in the contest already consume the days and nights of her life: Mom's living doll. How much more can she do to make The Mom happy? If you take The Stage and Pageant Mom as your lawful wedded wife, you will have to deal with the fallout from all this Mamma Drama and its effect on your children.

Ego-mommia
The Stage Mom projects her ego into her kids the way a ventriloquist throws his voice into a dummy. When her baby is on stage, she is standing there, in her mind, yearningly basking in the adulation of the audience. What many of these Moms fail to understand is just because a child stars in a movie, or lands a featured role in a series, or does a few commercials, doesn't mean that the industry is now ready to roll over and put that child and her on a pedestal. In the over-all scheme of the business, it's just a job. It's just a role or another beauty contest for which she has paid heavily in tickets and costumes. That's all. And the odds are, someone else will be coming along very soon to fill the shoes of the current hot kid actor or pageant winner. But these Moms go off the deep end when their children do not get the part or win the pageant. They feel personally rejected. This puts them in very bad moods, so you better stay out of their way. The child also feels like a miserable failure as Mom argues, shouts, and emotes in her outrage that she did not get her way with the judges the way she always has with you.

Soccer Mom
The Soccer Mom is easily identifiable by men and women alike. She is the one who wants to prove to the world that she is the best and most super of all the Super-moms that ever existed. She talks loudly in any social situation about how much she does for her kids so everyone will know what a saint she is for sacrificing her life for her

children. She is earning her ticket to Mommy Heaven with her list of activities she has planned for her children and the places she drives them. She thinks this list of endless activities passes for conversation. It goes like this: "I'm totally stressed out today. I had to take Timmy to soccer practice, Heather to dance, Jimmy to karate, then Heather is having a sleepover so we had to get special stuff for that and I had to get Timmy ready for soccer camp and take Jimmy to the doctor for his ear infection and then over to his friend Scott's birthday party and pick up the Girl Scout cookies, I'm Den Mother, you know, and then I've got to bake cookies for the bake sale. Where are you as a husband and lover in all this Mommy-mania?

Double Moms

The most difficult manifestation of The Mom is the one who teams up with her own Mom to form the dreaded Double Mom. Sometimes The Mom's Mom will actually move in with you after marriage. Her daughter is the center of her life and they spent hours on the phone with each other before she moved in. Now they are a team. You get both barrels as they attack you, either verbally, or by giving you the hairy eyeball when you walk into the room. They have been talking about what a human zero you were before they came into your life and what a complete nothing you are now, in spite of their best efforts. They watch you silently as you cross the room, waiting for you to do something wrong so they can look knowingly at each other to confirm their rightness. You feel like a motorist tailgated unnervingly by a police car. The red lights start flashing as you hear the Mom's Mom whisper, "See, I told you he was a spineless, good-for-nothing, no-talent loser when you introduced him to me, and he hasn't changed. He never was good enough for you! Look at how he hangs up his coat!"

THE MOM EXAMPLES

Mamma Knows Best

"Arthur! Come over here now! I said now!" Lily shouted. "You're worse than one of the kids! How many times do I have to tell you not to leave your coffee mug in the family room? Kids, look what Daddy did! Didn't I tell everyone to clean up his or her own mess? Well, guess what? Daddy didn't. So now Mommy has to clean up for him!"

Lily makes a great show of bringing the mug into the kitchen and washing it. Arthur protests that he wasn't finished drinking his coffee, had just gone to use the bathroom, and was going right back into the family room. The children are watching all of this.

Lily barks, "Don't look at me that way, Arthur! I don't want to hear your excuses, either. Excuses, excuses; that's all I get from you. You had an excuse last night when you were late from work. You have an excuse for why Wilson got promoted over you when you've been there longer. You've got an excuse for why you are in the same income bracket as you were two years ago! Kids, come over here and see Daddy try to squirm out of things with his excuses. No excuses are allowed in this household! Arthur, do you hear me? Answer me when I m talking to you! And stand up straight!"

Arthur walks sadly towards the bedroom to pack and leave. He catches a glimpse of his unhappy children in the corner of this eye. He flashes back to those college days when he was enticed by Lily's warm sensuality and womanliness. He admits she had been bossy then and always convinced of her rightness, but he enjoyed the times in bed and excused it as a sign that she knew her own mind and wasn't wishy-washy. He did not know enough about life then to predict that the good times they had would end up like this, with her constant criticism and emasculating remarks.

Stan's Little Helper

Stan and Cheri had been together only three months but she wanted to prove her domesticity and how well she could take care of him as a potential wife. She did this by going over to his house, cleaning it, and doing his chores for him, even though he never mentioned that he wanted this from her. He became annoyed one day when she came over and started cleaning up beer bottles left from last night s get-together with his friends. She was acting like his Mom, wiping his counters down for him, clucking, "My boy's just so messy! After I finish your kitchen, I'll do your laundry. I'm sure it needs to be done from the way that hamper is overflowing in your bedroom. I'll even teach you how to get your shirts out of the dryer while still damp so they won't be so wrinkled when you wear them. I've noticed that some of your shirts are very wrinkled. But don't worry, I'll iron them for you!"

When she finished her clean-up duties she came over to Stan to rub his back. Sensuous enjoyment of her massage softened his annoyance. He got very turned on and it looked like she was feeling the same. They raced to the bedroom and tore off their clothes. But just when they started to kiss, Cheri stopped to pick their clothes off the floor. She folded them and put them away in the closet! The mood was destroyed for Stan. They lay next to each other as she planned their future together. The last thing he heard before he sank into sleep was Cheri telling him what a great housekeeper she is and how happy she will make him.

CELEBRITY EXAMPLES OF THE MOM

Mom-like Behavior

Most celebrities do not display their Mom-like qualities to the public eye nor does Mom-like behavior draw headlines the way scandal does. No movie stars' publicists will allow them to display bossy, pushy behavior towards their boyfriends and husbands, even if they do so in their private lives. The Moms are easier to control in public than PMS Queens, whose tantrums give them away. Also, since the kids are the center of The Mom's life, having a full-time career as a celebrity is incompatible with Mom-like behavior. However, some celebrities' images are Mom-like to the general public. For example, Mia Farrow's compulsion to adopt babies from around the world is admirable, though some have found it obsessive. She is the mother of fourteen children; ten of whom she adopted; four of them have special needs. A husband, lover, or boyfriend might have difficulty scheduling time with her.

Dr. Laura

A clear example of the "I know better than you do," Mom is

Dr. Laura. Laura Schlessinger is the aggressive radio talk show host whose opinion reaches a daily audience of almost 20 million listeners. A mixture of Leona Helmsley and Tammy Faye Baker, Dr. Laura belts out a continuous stream of, in her own words, "preaching, teaching and nagging," on almost 500 radio stations in the U.S. and Canada. She can be confrontational and make the people seeking her advice feel small the way The Mom's husband is made to feel. She mocks and humiliates her callers, some of whom have serious problems.

Typical of The Mom, she thinks she can tell her callers everything they are doing wrong in their lives as if she is the messiah of good ol' family values and common sense. As hyper-mom, she is condescending to everyone who is not Dr. Laura.

Her callers, chosen from among tens of thousands of advice-seekers each week, describe the mess their lives have become: Bad marriages, bad relationships, and out-of-control children. Dr. Laura is happy to tell them they are "sickening," "selfish," "stupid," "gutless," "termites," or "pigs," and that they should "grow up!" She declares, "I'm my kid's mom" frequently. While she may think she is calling people names for their own good, like Mom spanking them for their mistakes, the pain may be stronger than the gain.

Kathy Lee

Kathy Lee Gifford is notorious for her sugar-sweet enshrinement of her child Cody. Poor, defenseless Cody was deified in front of millions daily during the late morning hours of television. Even her show partner, Regis, rolled his eyes in dismay as she yakked on and on about what Cody did that morning. However, her enviable motherly love and devotion was contradicted by the news that she used child labor in Central American sweat-shops to produce her clothing line.

PREVENTION: NOTICE BEHAVIOR

House Mom

Early on in the relationship you'll see how desperately she wants to prove how domestic she is and how well she can take care of you. That's great but she should not be going over to your house and cleaning up your place or doing your chores for you. This is an indication that she already does not trust you to take care of your own life right now in your own place. Notice if she acts like your wife or live-in girlfriend before she actually is either. She must remember, it is your house, and she is your guest. Notice if she acts like your maid and starts wiping your counters down for you just because, "Oh gosh you're just so messy, I'll just get that for you!" She is trying to be your little helper because Mamma knows best.

Control Freakiness

Notice how much of a backseat or front seat driver she is. Remember, The Mom thinks she is the only one who can do anything right, including driving the car. When you drive, notice if she is very nervous about people running into you and killing you. An example is: Every time a car changes lanes, her sharp, hissing intake of breath keeps you thinking that something bad is about to happen. She might scream out, "Watch out!" with such terror you think the car is on the brink of a cliff, when in reality the truck in front of you has merely turned on its blinker. When looking for a parking spot, she blames you because you didn't see the one she picked fast enough, someone else took it, and now you have to walk further to the store! In the store, she shows you that she knows how to shop better than you do and she has the coupons to prove it. The Mom finds it difficult to hide her need to control. It is a quality that predominates all her speech and actions.

Psycho Babbler

Verbal Diarrhea

TalkieTalk
The Psycho Babbler analyzes and dissects a relationship until it dies from dismemberment. She tends to overanalyze most things but particularly scrutinizes your relationship. She talks it to death, taking love's spontaneity and joy and pulling it apart, like a laboratory technician dissecting a specimen or a clumsy child pulling the wings off a butterfly to see what makes it fly. She wants to talk at great lengths about where you are going "with this thing," its ground rules, her feelings, your feelings, the world's feelings, your thoughts, her thoughts, long into the night. She usually wants to have "The Talk" early on in the relationship, usually after your first time in bed. "Are we exclusive? Are we committed yet?" Psycho Babbler wants to discuss these questions in detail, and apply psychoanalytic jargon to your situation.

Typical Scenario
You and your ladylove have just had multi-orgasmic sex. You are amazed at how euphoric you feel and appreciate her beauty. As you lie back to enjoy the afterglow, you close your eyes for a minute just to rest. You would like to share the moment in silence, or perhaps drift off into sleep in each other's arms. Then she starts talking to you. "Sweetie, that was fantastic! I hope it was good for you too! Was it Honey? Hello? Helloooooh! Honey, let's talk. You know, after all the jerks I've been dating and after being dumped more

times than I can count, I'm ready for a committed relationship and I just want to know how you feel about it. I mean, I need some sign from you that you are willing to commit to making this thing work and are on the same page as I am." She becomes teary-eyed because you do not answer right away. She wants you to describe exactly how you feel about her and is unhappy.

Psycho Analysis
You mumble that you think you are in love with her. She asks you to define "think." After you rally your brain and come up with some decent-sounding definitions, she asks you to define "love." When you sweat through defining it, she picks the definition apart and asks you to define each word in the definition. "So you love me the way you love your dog? I want more than that from the man in my life. Are you willing to commit to me? Can you be committed to me the way you are to your work? I mean, how much do you love me? I want to know exactly what you mean by that word! Right now I'm not feeling very special because of the way you're treating me. I need someone to be there for me and to understand my moods and feelings. I need to talk!" The afterglow vanishes, replaced by the spotlight of her Gestapo questioning. You feel like committing her!

Analyze This!
"What happened to you when you were a child that makes you shut down like this?" She now wants to discuss some-thing you told her about your childhood last night, when she was cross-examining you about your feelings. She tells you she is beginning to understand why you act the way you do. Your abandonment issues keep you from being

emotionally available to her. You are afraid of being abandoned yourself, so you are afraid to commit to her to avoid the pain of it all just in case she decides to abandon you first, which she would never do because she has her own abandonment issues and understands what it feels like to be abandoned. You drift off to sleep as she psychoanalyzes you into oblivion, but she does not let you sleep for long. She has other things she needs to discuss with you.

A Psycho, A Babbler
Spending a quiet evening with Psycho Babbler is impossible. She cannot abide silence for too long. She proves the truism, "Nature abhors a vacuum," by filling up every moment with talk. Furthermore, the talk tends to be intrusive and judgmental, usually of you and of how much counseling you need. Her other favorite topic is her ever-changing self and how much counseling she is getting. Psycho Babblers put enormous faith in their counselors and think the rest of the world, including you, is in denial because it is not seeking help. They also believe that all people who do not think and behave the way they want them to, are sick and need psychoanalysis.

Sex Therapy
An acquaintance of mine, Galinda, is an example of one style of Psycho Babbler. She insists on taking all new boyfriends to sex therapy early on in the relationship. If they do not comply, they are automatically out. She told me a story about a man she had been dating. He was an intriguing New Zealander, a combination of refinement and athleticism, with an interest in a wide range of subjects. He was in his forties and had traveled the world as an art dealer

and collector. Her friends congratulated her. He was a good catch. After they made love for the first time, she looked into his eyes and asked, "Was it good for you?" He answered, "Yes, you were great beyond description! It was better than I even imagined with all my soul's yearning!" She replied, "Well, that's not my idea of good sex. Either we see a sex therapist together or this relationship is over tonight!" For the rest of the evening, Galinda took apart his performance, like a sports commentator at the Super Bowl, showing classic Psycho Babbler style.

Me, Me, Me, Me, Me
The Psycho Babbler pretends to be interested in what you are thinking, so she can analyze it. In reality she only wants certain responses from you about her. She wants to hear that you will never leave her because nobody could ever love you the way she does or would be as beautiful. She wants you to listen to her endlessly about her inconsequential little self-centered life, and if you do not conform to her wishes, you are the one with problems. The world revolves around her and she wants to control what you say and think about her. Because her major preoccupation is herself, she can put in large amounts of time at the psychiatrist's office. That is her refuge where she can talk about herself and have her every move and thought analyzed for as long as her money or HMO holds out.

TELL-ALL-ITIS

Spewing
The Psycho Babbler must talk at all costs and eventually she

will want to tell you everything she ever did before she met you. This includes her high school lesbian experiences, how she used to skip school, and whom she used to sleep with. She tells it all. Maybe you do not want to hear that your sweet little Angel had a drunken hardcore sex session with her 40-year old neighbor on graduation day. Maybe you do not really want to know that your darling innocent girlfriend had a threesome in the basement of Bill's Sporting Goods or that she racked up 120 notches on her bedpost before you came into her life. Nevertheless, she thinks it is necessary to list and rate every man that came before you. And that's not all. After a half-hour list of names and scores ("Sam was the best. He could lick me for three hours. He had a dick like the Titanic!"), she wraps up the whole monologue with, "But you're so much better than any one of those 120 men I was with before. Really!"

Landmine Questions

Some Psycho Babblers do not stop at blurting out their own experiences. They also want you to tell them about every one of your exes and rate them too. You are entering a field of landmines. They say they want to know, "How many were there before me-me-me-me-me? What were they like?" When you tell them, be prepared for a negative and sulky reaction. Any woman who wants to destroy her sense of self-worth by hearing the truth about how great Cindy was between the sheets, and that Sandra had the best breasts on the planet, or what a sex-machine that nympho Carla was, is asking for it. Engaging in such descriptions will set off explosions, even though she has asked for it. You will not drift off to sleep quietly after such revelations.

Woman from Mars

Sometimes the Psycho Babbler can be entertaining, though unfathomable. She wants you to understand completely how she feels about the relationship. She might perform an interpretive dance to explain her emotions. Or she will read her poetry aloud. She wants to make artistic displays about her intensity. A celebrity example of this type might be Angelina Jolie. She sports several scars from playing with knives (including an X on her arm, a slice on her stomach, and a nick on her neck), or as she puts it "You're young, you're drunk, you're in bed, you have knives; shit happens." When she married Jonny Lee Miller in 1995, she wore a white shirt with her husband's name painted across the back, in her own blood. She also insisted on wearing a vial of Billy Bob Thornton's blood around her neck when she was married to him.

She had written "To the end of time," in her blood and framed it to hang over their bed. The end of time came quickly enough when their marriage dissolved.

Psycho Babbler Moms

Self-help Mom

When Psycho Babblers become moms, they are self-help obsessed in their quest to raise a psychologically liberated child. They will often let their kids run wild because they believe in "creativity" and letting children "express themselves." As their father, if you try to correct your difficult and out-of-control kiddies, she will stop you and give you a lecture something like this: "We don't say 'No' in this household. You must show these children immense respect, openness, and interest as to why the Universe has brought these small persons into our lives and what they are here to teach us."

Explanations

Instead of directing a young child's behavior, the Psycho Babbler mom will give reasons and explanations for simple tasks. She bargains with the child even to get dressed in the morning or to go out, to pick up after himself or to get through a store without buying a toy. She cares more about the children's feelings than about their behavior, and as a result is afraid to set boundaries that restrict their feelings of empowerment. Focusing the family around the children's every need gives kids a hugely inflated sense of their own power that devalues you as a dad. Mom has taught them that they are God's gift to the Earth. Later, they will be in for a shock when they find out the rest of the world doesn't feel that way and won't give into or understand their screaming tantrums. So you are not doing your progeny a favor by combining your sperm with a Psycho Babbler mom's eggs.

PSYCHO BABBLER EXAMPLES

Talkathon

Lennie told me this story, "A few years back I picked up a woman for a blind date. From the moment she got in the car, she was talking about herself. She was talking and talking and talking and talking. . . I didn't even have to be there--it was a monologue. We drove into town, parked, and went into the restaurant. After we were seated, I realized, she was still talking about herself - there was no end in sight, and she had no apparent interest in me. The waiter tried to take our orders several times, but she hadn't even looked at her menu because she was too busy talking. She was like the Energizer Bunny! Finally I interrupted her to let her know the waiter was approaching for the fourth time. She hastily looked at the menu and ordered a burger - despite the fact that this was a somewhat classy steak house. Well, they brought her meal out - the burger was open-faced. She was so busy talking and not paying attention that when she put the two halves of the bun together and tried to take a bite, the burger slipped out - right into her lap!

"She was dabbing at the grease on her dress when she looked up at me and said, 'I like the chemistry between us. What do you see for our future together? I'm a serious person and need someone who will be there for me when I need him to listen to and understand me.' She continued to talk about 'Our relationship' for the rest of the night, including in the car while I drove her home.

"As I said goodbye to her, she said, 'I'm so glad you opened up to me. I learned so much about you. What are we doing tomorrow night? I was thinking it would be good to start out on the right foot and see my counselor Ramona together. I know she has an opening tomorrow night because I see her every Tuesday, Thursday, and Saturday. Then we might go back to that restaurant where we were tonight. I really liked their burgers!'"

Psycho Babbler Magnet

Noah told me his story, one night over dinner. "I've always attracted Psycho Babbler chicks. One wanted to show me the razor cuts on her arms after hours of telling me about her years of therapy. Another called and hung up repeatedly the first month I knew her because, she said later, I had a communication problem and she wanted me to see what it felt like to be cut off. That same one sprayed mace all over me in an argument because she said I wasn't listening to her and she wanted to get my attention. A different one took me to Couple's Training after the first week. Most of these chicks were in therapy several days a week. Two actually were therapists.

"Here's an example: Dee-Dee came up to me in a New York bar and asked for a cigarette, but said she didn't smoke. As she was smoking the cigarette she said she didn't smoke, she told me she was suing her husband. He had tried to have her committed. She wanted to run away to Afghanistan with me tonight. I mentioned they were killing people there. I weakened and told her she could stay with me for the night. She stayed up until three a.m. singing to the night through an open window. I had a hard time shutting her up. I'm beginning to wonder: What is it about me that attracts these kinds of women?"

Soul Sister

Phil thought it would be fun to look up one of his old friends, Cassandra, during his vacation in New York City, where he once lived. They decided to meet in an old hangout and have drinks. After a few scotches they began to kiss. Soon neither of them came up for air as they engaged in an endless lip-lock. Cassandra invited Phil to continue their discussion at her place. Phil agreed. It was getting late and closing time was approaching.

They arrived at her place and barely made it through the door when they pounced on and devoured each other. When it was over, they lay on the floor and talked for a while. Then Phil got up to go back to his hotel. He had a full schedule the next day and wanted to sleep, shower, and change clothes. Cassandra pulled him down next to her, "I can't believe that you are getting up and leaving after what we just shared. Don't you understand that our destinies are bound inextricably for eternity now that we have shared our love? Don't you understand that the forces of the universe brought us together on the checkerboard of life and we are united in soul and spirit for infinity? Do you think you can shirk your responsibility and go off and shower and shave just as if nothing happened? Worlds have collided, souls have intermingled, and you want to leave? Let me read you a poem I wrote yesterday in anticipation of our union:

"Yo Phil, Incarnation of the Divine Essence,
Fill me with your spiritual quintessence!
Bathe me in the glow of your Karma.
Let me feel the weight of your Dharma.
Our destinies are intertwined interminably
In the esoteric synchronicity of spirituality!"

Phil was dumbfounded by Cassandra's intensity. This little get-together had gotten way out of hand. He thought it was going to be a casual night of reminiscences about old times. He felt trapped. He regretted that his brain had been in the back seat and the booze had done the driving. But every time he got up to leave, Cassandra pulled him down to her again. "Phil, don't you understand that you cannot leave me? Even though your body might be away from me, your soul is still with me! So don't even try to get away. You are mine for life!"

Phil desperately searched his mind for a way out of the mess he had created. Finally he said, "If indeed my spirit is with you always, it doesn't matter if I am physically here with you or not. I can be in my hotel room shaving and I am still with you, so, hasta la vista, baby. I'll see you in eternity!"

CELEBRITY PSYCHO BABBLER EXAMPLES

Monica

The gushing Psycho Babblerish utterances of Monica Lewinsky about being Billy Clinton's sexual soul mate are prime examples of a celebrity attempting to sound profound while merely sounding ludicrous. Often newscasters will inquire of some starlet, singer, or Valley Girl bimbette about the state of the world. What qualifies these ladies to be experts and wise women with real answers? Usually their answers are full of cliches about loving yourself before you can love anyone else and learning to love themselves more.

Monica's affair with the President was not just another episode in the squalid Clintonian sexual saga: "We were soul mates!" She claims that her neurotic entanglement with the prez shows that "I am comfortable with my sexuality."

She speaks of Bill Clinton's reluctance to move beyond his preferred non-coital method of sexual congress as "discomfort with his own sexuality" and sees it as the result of his "religious upbringing." She swore to Billy Boy that she would never reveal their affair, and then, in the verbally diarrheic style of the Psycho Babbler, quite casually shared with numerous girlfriends (even apart from the infamous Linda Tripp) the sordid details of her presidential "relationship." She still, for the life of her, cannot understand why everyone made such a big deal about a little thing like his lying under oath.

In true Psycho Babbler fashion Monica translates an under-the-desk blow job while Billy was on the phone dealing with the Bosnian situation, into an encounter with the deepest levels of her soul, her karma and her destiny. She turns the incident with the cigar into a spiritual epiphany. It is all high drama in her fabulously important quest for love. Meanwhile, Mr. Clinton claimed he did not remember ever being in the same room with Monica Lewinsky. He was an onlooker. In other words, he was just standing there - taking it all in, while she was kneeling there - taking it all in. He himself did not participate. Yet it was a great soul encounter. She said, "I know people make fun of him for having said, 'I feel your pain,' but I think he genuinely means it. The first time I remember was when he talked about the loss of the American soldier in Bosnia."

Monica's pre-Clintonian behavior also qualifies her as a Psycho Babbler. She once kept an affair going with a married teacher (Andy J. Bleiler) in her high school after he wanted to stop it. She threatened to tell his wife and stalked him through the mail. Mr. Bleiler said that Monica had called him as often as four or five times a day after coming to Washington in 1995 as a White House intern, and that she talked obsessively about sex, including boasts that she was involved in a sexual relationship with a "high ranking White House official." Bleiler said their relationship finally ended after his wife found out about it, when word filtered back to her through Lewinsky's bragging to former college acquaintances. Psycho Babblers have difficulty keeping their mouths shut.

During her trial she said, "For the last ten months I have seen the Special Prosecutor, the press, the White House and the public ripping apart layer upon layer of my soul. I don't know what I did to deserve that humiliation. Certainly I made mistakes and foolish judgments, but did they warrant this level of abuse? Yes, I probably am the most humiliated woman in the world, but I just can't deal with that thought. I have to block it out because it is too much to handle!" Let's hope the $6 million advance she got for her tell-all book will help her deal with it.

Angelina and Madness
Before Angelina Jolie's and Billy Bob Thornton's marriage came to an abrupt halt, they adopted a Cambodian baby that they named "Maddox," and calling him, appropriately enough, "Madness." Poor Baby Madness was plucked from his perfectly good third-world shantytown to be dropped into a maelstrom of Hollywood neuroses. Sure, he came from Cambodia -- home of abject poverty, political killings, abysmal working conditions, and former land of the Khmer Rouge. But faced with the terrifying alternative of

calling Angelina Jolie "Mommy," he might have been better off staying and taking his chances in the killing fields. As Jolie told the Internet Movie Database, "This is going to sound insane, but there was a time I was going to hire somebody to kill me."

It is well known that Jolie has cultivated a unique set of interests and is not afraid to talk about them. She aspired to be a funeral director, read widely about Vlad the Impaler, and nursed a crush on Spock (the Vulcan). Reality was always something of a letdown. As Jolie told one interviewer, "I remember being very upset that I wasn't crazy, that I wasn't a vampire." Her penchant for talking about her now-defunct love affair with Billy Bob, produced such lines as: "Like a lot of couples, you always talk about how much in love with each other you are, and you can't think of enough ways to devour each other and take each other. And blood is your life. So many times, I have just wanted to drink every part of him."

PREVENTION: LISTENING SKILLS

Listen Up

Psycho Babblers give you a clue early on that they are non-stop talkers with an insatiable need to express themselves to you. You do not have to be a master detective to understand that if a woman behaves this way on the first and second date, she will not get less psycho-like later in life. Her compulsion to tell all that is on her mind until it has been drained of its excretions is a lifelong pursuit. Ask yourself if you can live with this type of filibuster. If you are a shy man you might find relief that you do not have to do much of the talking. But you have to think long-term. How much strange behavior can you take over the years?

The Babbling Brook

Listen to the content of the trendy words she is using. It is often pseudo-intellectual psycho-prattle designed to fool you into thinking that something intelligent is actually happening. But it's not. She is fascinated by easy-sounding and unscientifically proven formulas for why things are the way they are. And woe betide you if you are politically incorrect in any of your answers to her landmine questions! She might say she is a pacifist but if you question her sappy wisdom because she sounds a like a bumper sticker on a hippiemobile, she will turn on you with the rage of a PMS-Queen fueled by nitro. She will give you a meaning-of-life lecture that sounds like a inspirational greeting card combined with the Commandments, dispensing righteous-ness and whipping you back into place.

Use Your Brain

While it's true that logic will take you only so far in life, there's also something to be said for taking full advantage of those most blessed gifts, common sense and intellect. These two faculties will tell you that the Psycho Babbler is a no-winner. If you listen with a logical mind and have the patience to endure her non-stop analysis, you will see, that like all the Dirty Seven Sisters, she will make your life miserable. She may be the sexiest tigress in bed and you can be easily tempted by her intensity. But do not succumb. Her wildness might be a preview of future lack of self-control that is not so sexy in massive doses.

Men Don't Leave

If you think you can just hang around a Psycho Babbler for the sex and leave afterwards, you are a fool. Especially if you do so without explaining or try to forestall her by saying you will call her with no intention of doing so. She will come over to your prized automobile and smash the windshield or slash your tires to demonstrate the pain you have caused her. They are only material objects anyway compared to her flesh-and-blood heart! Nobody just walks out on a Psycho Babbler and you've got a lot of explaining to do. She wants to know every reason why you no longer see her and she will interpret it all as your own constipated inability to love anything or anyone in life. She will use words like, "You're sick, you need help," demonstrating her blind faith that counseling will solve everything.

Explain!

Be prepared to go through the hassles of changing your telephone number to deter her from calling you for an explanation. It is easier for you to nip a relationship with a Psycho Babbler in the bud by recognizing her type up front than to allow your contact with her to go on long enough for her to think you have bonded for life and that you "complete" her. Short of that, it is easier for you to explain why it isn't working out and take the blame for the breakup than it is to endure months, and possibly years, of being pursued for an explanation. Something like this works: "Yes, I am an unfeeling, cowardly, ridiculous worm who has no right to take up air space on this planet. Let me not pollute your aura any longer with my emotionally illiterate carcass. I have learned much from our encounter and will be eternally grateful to you."

KEEPERS

THE MINORITY

The majority of women are not Dirty Seven Sisters. Years of research and observation lead me to conclude that only ten percent of women qualify, with the largest concentration in the United States and other post-industrial nations. In the Third World and developing countries, where women are more concerned with enough grain for their next meal, the luxuries that enable Pretty Pennie, Thingie Wingie, The Material Girl, and The Wedding Belle to be the way they are, are not available. These spoiled, empty little purchasing machines can be the way they are because of the abundance of consumer goods in modern society. Other blood-sucking types like Needee Nellie would be too busy trying to fill her empty bellies and those of their children before trying to fill the emptiness of their life with male companionship.

WOMEN'S RIGHTS

In some ways, the emergence of women's rights also allowed the emergence of the Dirty Seven Sisters. Where women have no rights, any behavior that is not polite, obedient, and modest is subject to punishment or death. The alimony-grabbing Material Girl would not thrive in parts of the world where men have several wives and receive dowries from the girls families as an inducement to marry. In such parts of the world, a Needee Nellie following a man around and throwing herself at him would be a rarity. In countries where women are less-than-second-class citizens, the Psycho Babbler would be socialized to be quiet on penalty of extermination. The PMS Queen would be publicly executed. Cultures where males dominate and women have no rights don't tolerate The Mom's disrespect to her spouse nor Shopaholica's user tactics and flirtatious ways.

DIRTY SEVEN SISTER INCLINATIONS

Though no laboratory studies exist, my experience dictates that ninety percent of women are not members of the Dirty Seven Sisters sorority to any alarming degree, though all may have inclinations towards one type or another. You may see streaks of The Mom in someone who tends to be bossy, and hints of Pretty Pennie in a girl who is overly conscious of appearances. A woman may be moody occasionally but she rarely goes to the extremes of the PMS Queen. Sometimes a woman will go through a cycle in which she acts clingy and needy but these behaviors are not underlying personality traits that drive her activities every day of the year as they do with Needee Nellie. Some females may want to have "The Talk," but not as insistently or as repeatedly as the Psycho Babbler does. Others may go over the top with enthusiasm about their weddings but have other things going on in their lives besides reading and re-reading *Brides* magazine from cover to cover.

THE GOOD, THE BETTER, AND THE BEAUTIFUL

Good mates, girlfriends, lovers, and wives exhibit the opposite traits of the Dirty Seven Sisters. These women abound and outnumber their evil twins by far. They are as follows:

- **The non-PMS Queen:** She has enough self control and understanding of others to know that stomping around and having temper tantrums are ineffective ways of getting what she wants. Even if she is not feeling well she shows kindness and patience towards others. If she does have her period, she realizes that she not the only woman in the world who menstruates. She does not use it as an excuse for inflicting psychological pain on anyone. She is humble and does not act like a queen to whom all her subjects must bow and obey her every whim. She understands that if she wants something from her mate, she must communicate it and not expect him to read her mind.

- **The non-Needee Nellie:** She has a full life of her own in which she contributes value to the people around her. She does not throw her body at a man in hopes that he will take the bait and stay with her eternally. She is with you because she enjoys your company, not because she wants you to be her savior.

- **The un-Material Girl:** She is interested in you, not what she can get from you. There is more to her life than self-decoration, material goods, and money. She thinks about ideas and is capable conversations about a range of topics other than the next object she wants to acquire. When the relationship ends, she does not try to drain you financially so you can support her in her life of ease.

- **The non-Shopaholica:** She is really with you when she is with you. She is happy with who you are and lets you know it. Her eyes are on you when you are out in public, not on every other guy in the room. She wants to be with you because she loves you romantically and she knows that it is insulting to flirt with or talk about how hot some other guy is while letting you know that you do not measure up.

- **The non-Wedding Belle:** She is more interested in you when she first meets you than what your future together will be. She has self-confidence and happiness in her own life. She does not hope for an elaborate wedding to make all her dreams come true. Her feet are grounded in reality. She realizes that many times fantasy weddings are soon followed by divorce because the spectacle was all show and no substance. She understands that the union between people is a contract of the heart for which ceremony is no replacement. After marriage, she does not let herself go because she has now accomplished her goal. She continues to keep herself sexy and lovable, devoted and caring.

- **The non-Mom:** She trusts your judgment and treats you with respect as an intelligent being. She keeps herself sexually interesting to you. She is more interested in getting along well with you than in proving that she is right all the time.

- **The non-Psycho Babbler:** She is lighthearted about romance and love. She does not insist on talking about the relationship too soon. If things do not work out, she is willing to go her own way with confidence that she will find someone more compatible. She does not stalk you, ask for hundreds of explanations, blame you, threaten you, or make a general pain in your life out of herself. She can be quiet and be happy at the same time. She has an inner core of peace and wisdom and enjoys shared, comfortable silence with you.

Questions and Answers

Post-traumatic Relationship Syndrome (PRS)

I've had so many bad relationships with women I'm beginning to think that they are the incarnation of evil itself. I'm better off with my one-hand magazines and a couple of beers or even a prostitute, so I won't have to deal with the emotional roller coasters that I've gotten from the women in my life. Help!

Men have told me hundreds of stories of girlfriends running amok, making them fear the dating scene and cower in the safety of their rooms. They suffer from Post-traumatic Relationship Syndrome (PRS). Their experiences of one, two, or all of the Dirty Seven Sisters cause them to generalize that all women are selfish, irrational, emotion-driven machines of consumption and frivolity, neediness and manipulation. Yet independent, admirable, intelligent, kind, beautiful, funny and fun-loving women are all around us. It takes patience and a sense of purpose to find one, unlike what transpires on today's television dating shows, where interest is based purely on perfection of face and body or size of booty or mammary glands.

It is important to be aware of the bait and switch tactics of the Dirty Seven Sisters but this does not mean you must shy away from all women forever. Often, even when a man's internal alarm bells go off, he pursues, or allows himself to be pursued by, someone he knows is not right for him. This is like spending time test-driving cars that you know are not for you. It is ironic that some men spend more time selecting their automobiles than they do choosing their female companions. Then they wonder why things go sour later. They would not bring home a lemon from the dealership, thinking that it will somehow get better with time. The Dirty Seven Sisters are like lemons. They may sport a shiny new coat of paint, but they still cause problems down the line. However, to shy away from driving cars forever because you had a bad experience with a few is just as silly as thinking that all women are evil because you have been burned a few times.

Search yourself and discover why you allowed your crazy relationship to go on so long when you weren't happy with the way things were going. Was it because of the sex and you were too lazy to go out and find someone more compatible? That is often the case.

The Good, the Bad, and the Dirty

What are the qualities I should be looking for in a woman if I don't want to end up with one of the Dirty Seven Sisters?

ॐ

The same qualities that make for a good all-around human being apply to a good mate, with the added value of sex appeal. If you look for the following qualities, you are sure to pick a winner:

1. **Common sense:** Though ditziness can be funny, and make you feel superior and manly, over the long term

it is a wearying quality that makes you feel you cannot depend on her to be reasonable. The only way you can determine if a woman has common sense is by observing her over time. What are her responses to life's difficult moments? Is she flaky or responsible?

2. **Emotional warmth and kindness:** All of the Dirty Seven Sisters are lacking in these qualities in some way. Needee Nellies, PMS Queens, and Psycho Babblers are hyper-emotional and unbalanced on the heated end of the spectrum. Shopaholicas, Material Girls, Wedding Belles, and The Mom are unbalanced on the colder end of the emotional spectrum, sometimes lacking feeling of any kind at all except for enthusiasm for things, not people. The only one of the Dirty Seven Sisters who shows any kindness is Needee Nellie and she goes overboard with it, turning it into a sticky-sweet bog of emotional quicksand. None of the others, in their self-interest, display warmth or kindness to any degree.

3. **Sense of humor:** None of the Dirty Seven Sisters has the ability to laugh with any kind of enjoyment, especially at themselves. The Psycho Babbler especially takes herself overly seriously. Material Girls are hell-bent on their possessions, which they clutch onto with humorless white knuckles. The Mom is too busy being right and proving you wrong to lighten up. The only laughter you will get from her is derisive. The PMS Queen grouses and quarrels instead of experiencing happiness and levity. Her laugh is one of bitter irony and self-pity. Needy Nellie is so intense, she cries more than she laughs. If she does laugh, it is too loud

and too long at a joke that does not warrant such an extreme response. In her hopes of obtaining your approval, she will turn herself inside out laughing at your merest jokes.

Does she come across as hard-to-please and easily bored? Does she get into arguments easily? Is she depressed and sad much of the time? Does she have frequent emotional upsets? Is she sarcastic and cynical and hardly ever smiles? Things will not improve over the years if they are already this bad at the beginning with the humorless Dirty Seven Sisters.

4. **Character:** This is another attribute that you can only determine over time. Can she handle adversity or does she fall apart in hysterics like the PMS Queen, Psycho Babbler, and Needee Nellie? Do you feel respect for her substance as a person or is she shallow like Prettie Pennie, Gimmie Monie, and Thingie Wingie? Will she turn crazy on you and destroy property and privacy like the Psycho Babbler? These are questions you must ask yourself before you share bodily fluids and exchange commitments.

5. **Public behavior:** Is she rude to waiters and waitresses? If she can be cruel to a stranger, she can be even crueler to you. Or, like Shopaholica, does she flirt with them instead? Does she have a violent temper or complain too often? Is she loud and obnoxious in public? Does she fling herself at other men when she is out with you or point out all the men she thinks are good-looking?

Does she create an embarrassing scene in public? The Mom, The Psycho Babbler, and the PMS Queen especially, will have public fits, usually in an attempt to make you look stupid. Needee Nellie will get sloppy drunk and plaster you with kisses, like the little PDA-hog that she is. She will refer to you as her boyfriend after the second date, stare at you as if you were the last man on earth, and use baby talk inappropriately in front of your friends and strangers.

6. **Courtesy and conversation:** Does she order the most expensive item on the menu every time? This is something all categories of Material Girl will do. She will also talk about how many credit cards she has and what a big shopper she is. She will talk about the dream house and lifestyle that you know you cannot afford. Or, like the Wedding Belle, does she talk about her dream wedding, which costs more than a college education for four? Pay attention to all of these warning signs.

Does she show that she is a good listener? Does she interrupt you continuously when you are talking? Does she accept calls and talk too long on the cell phone (probably to another man) while she is out with you (like Shopaholica)? Does she talk too much altogether? Does she ask you questions and not wait for the answer before she offers her opinion? Does she tell you you are wrong much of the time, without listening to your explanations?

These are just some of the questions you must ask yourself if you want to avoid pain and aggravation in your relationships. Leaving it all up to chance and sexual desperation is a mistake that you will regret for many years ahead.

Aren't Psycho Chicks Better in Bed?

I have dated psycho chicks and regular girls and the nut jobs are definitely better in bed, even though they are a pain in the nether regions during the rest of the time I am with them.

ॐ

I asked some male friends about this. According to my friend DP, "It's true, crazy psycho chicks are the best in bed! Good girls like to party, and sometimes can be terrific lovers, but they worry about things like, 'Will he respect me in the morning?' and 'Am I acting like a slut?' Bad girls drink straight from the whiskey bottle, dress like 42nd Street hookers, and are straight up slutty and wild in the sack. They are unpredictable and dangerous. Give me that wild, out-of-control woman every time!"

However, many men disagree. My friend RD counters with: "A nice normal girl can be just as sexually adventurous and enthusiastic in bed as anyone else. Psycho girlfriends can be just as horrible in bed as they are in a relationship or on a date. I've dated both, and the nice normal girl I'm seeing now is incredible, while another super crazy girl I dated howls at the moon and talks to flowers like Hamlet's Ophelia. She was the worst lay I ever had."

Just because a female is responsible, considerate, and

nice, doesn't mean she has to be boring in bed. Nice men also suffer from this same prejudice, as in the saying, "Nice men finish last." (Finishing last can be a good thing in certain circumstances.) Men have told me that conservative-looking, educated girls are the most creative in bed because they are intelligent and imaginative. They have also told me that some of the most provocatively dressed girls, with globes of silicon jiggling and bared to the nipple, are actually dead fish in bed. Their breasts are as hard as bowling balls, just like their personalities. This is why it is not a good thing to make generalizations based on looks. Behavior is the only true indicator of the mateability of a woman.

Observe behavior and do not be fooled by surfaces. Too many men have been taken in by the fantasy, thinking it is more exciting than the reality of a nice girl. Know the difference between someone with whom you could spend time happily and someone who drives you to despair, boredom, and angst.

Don't People Keep Making the Same Mistakes?

I've noticed that my friends and I keep picking the same kinds of women, even if they are not good for us. Even after reading your book, I am still drawn to women who start out being fun and end up being one giant quagmire of need. My best friend, for example, keeps falling for The Mom. All his girlfriends put him down in public and make him look stupid.

ॐ

Sometimes we intellectually recognize that something or someone is not good for us, but we continue in the same pattern. I do not think anyone who injects heroine in an alleyway thinks it is a good and healthy thing to do, but he or she does it anyway because it is an addiction. Addictions and compulsions are difficult to break and the topic is beyond the range of this book. Choosing one of the Dirty Seven Sisters repeatedly is like betting on a sports team that loses every game. It doesn't make sense, but some men will continue to place money on losing teams because they hope that one day their luck will change. These girls are not going to change, no matter how patient you may be. Like a team full of untalented, lackadaisical players, they are not winners and if you choose them, you will be the loser.

Who's Boss?

In my culture we insist that it must be the man who dominates a relationship. The Dirty Seven Sisters would not even exist if there were one boss in a relationship: The Man! It is a blight of modern civilizations that women are allowed to behave in such a manner as you describe in this book. That is why some of the great civilizations have arranged marriages in which the woman has no choice. She must obey, be silent, and behave modestly. If she does not behave in this way she is severely punished, publicly beaten, stoned to death, or subjected to house arrest. That would put an end to the Dirty Seven Sisters!

❧

You are right. We can beat and oppress women who are inclined to show characteristics of the Dirty Seven Sisters to get them in line. But since that is illegal in some civilizations, the next best thing to do is to avoid them altogether and choose one of the many women who are capable of being companions, not mere chattel.

Psycho Bimbos: Why Do I Have to Suffer?

I feel for the men having to deal with the psycho girls from hell. I am a woman who has many male friends. And of course every once in a while they get mixed up with the psycho bitches that give all women a bad name. But all I have to say is - what about us friends? We bear the brunt of the psycho onslaught also. We are collateral damage! I have received numerous calls and threats from these psycho bimbos.

One case in point is my ex-friend Darrell (yes an ex-friend because of a psycho bimbo). His psycho bimbo decided, out of the blue, that Darrell was in love with me. She then decided to ruin my life by messing with my boyfriend and me. She went so far as to hack into our e-mail accounts and send unwanted mail accusing me of all sorts of activities with Darrell. I now no longer speak to Darrell, which is sad because we were friends for ten years!

Another case in point: My friend Doug got involved with a psycho girl who picked a fight with a man who was very large and very drunk. When Doug tried to save her, the big man stabbed him! She wasn't even sorry it happened. What is in the mind of these men that makes them pick these girls? I understand from my male friends that psychos are the best in bed, but come on, sex isn't worth getting stabbed and losing your friends!

It is unfortunate that the Dirty Seven Sisters give all women a bad name. The majority of women are trying to be good people and do not deserve to be blamed for the malfeasance of the minority. The Dirty Seven Sisters are not good people to be around because of certain personality defects. It is difficult to share life with them because of their selfishness. If they were men, they'd be intolerable too.

You ask, "What's in the mind of these men that makes them pick these girls?" Often these men are not thinking with their minds. They allow various other organs to think for them. The PMS Queen can be sexually stimulating in her passionate intensity. Needee Nellie can provoke pity and nurturing behavior in certain men as she fulfills their every sexual need. Some men have a Mommy Complex and enjoy the taunting domination of The Mom. Some men like the heartless, mercenary qualities of the Material Girls. It's a boost to their egos to be seen with Prettie Pennie. She can be a costly decorative object like the latest status symbol. The shallow man, whose life revolves around acquiring stuff, enjoys the endless pursuit of material objects that is Thingie Wingie's world.

Are Women Pure Evil?

I firmly believe all PURE evil can, in and of itself, be traced back to the source: a woman. This does not mean I do not enjoy using them for what they are worth, a lay, and truthfully I cannot help but pursue and conquer women. MAYBE even an occasional relationship, or should I say, what I want them to believe is a relationship until they bore me with their pathetic attempts at changing me, all the while screwing someone else while just having me on the backburner as a challenge.

છ

It sounds like you are a casualty of a Shopaholica and you are lashing out at all women. If it weren't for a woman, your mother, you would not be around to voice your opinion about women being the source of pure evil. By further logical extension, you are calling yourself "pure evil" because your source is a woman. With your attitude, I can see why you have been having women-troubles. If you think the only thing women are good for is a lay, you will be treated accordingly.

Are You a Wimp?
Your ex or current girlfriend, or wife, treats you like trash. She constantly offends you, intrudes in your life, makes your life miserable, destroys your friendships, threatens you, embarrasses you, degrades you, strips you of dignity and self worth, disrespects you and destroys your manliness to the point of making you a poor spineless shadow of a creature. Yet, you walk on eggshells around her and fear her as if she were some grandiose worthy enemy looming over you. There may be people with actual power and extremely high intelligence that you might have to deal with, both professionally and personally one day. What will you do then? Recoil, tremble, and cringe as they walk right over you? I'm tired of seeing men putting up with these female tyrants! Are you a bunch of wimps?

The Battered Wife Syndrome extends to men too. Some men may have such low self-esteem, they do not think they deserve anything or anyone better than what they have now, even if that person makes their life hell. I do not address the psychological problems that keep men in a holding pattern with disruptive or cold-hearted women. It seems, to the rational mind, that a man can stop being with a Dirty Seven Sister any time he chooses. She is not holding a physical gun to his head. He is in a prison of his own making. He allows her to manipulate him by not taking decisive action to end the harassment.

Why Do Women Bait and Switch?

I get tired of how a woman will let herself go once she feels comfortable with me. I can really relate to the bait and switch image you are talking about in the book. In my view, there are three levels in most relationships (1) When a lady belches or farts she gets embarrassed and excuses herself or apologizes. (2) When she begins to feel comfortable using and setting up new charge accounts in your name without feeling any guilt. As a matter of fact, she seems to be smiling all the time. (3) When a lady feels comfortable enough to hold a conversation with you while she is sitting on the potty taking a dump. Another aspect of (3) is when you want some peace and quiet and go to the john, she will corner you while you're sitting on the pot to tell you her opinion, no matter what! I don't know why this happens to me, but if a lady moves into my place and is my lady, the relationship changes. I believe it's called the battle of the sexes!

You have a point about the annoying habits of some women, in this case, crossing over boundaries and invading the bathroom to continue an argument. That is poor woman-to-woman behavior and is no less so with a man. I address the kinds of annoying habits that some women display in another chapter. However, just because a woman has a few annoying traits doesn't mean she is one of the Dirty Seven Sisters. As you mentioned, sometimes a woman will let herself behave badly once she feels secure about her status in a man's life. She has baited and switched, is not on her best behavior any more, and becomes comfortable with being rude, counting on the man's unconditional love.

So, What Else Is New?
Although you seem to think that this book is somehow going to educate the masses of naive or unsuspecting men out there, I beg to differ. How about *Fatal Attraction, The Hand that Rocks the Cradle, The Crush, Disclosure, Swimfan, Romeo is Bleeding, Single White Female, Body Heat, Double Indemnity,* etc., etc., etc?

The Dirty Seven Sisters are not criminals who murder and maim with ice picks while laughing diabolically. They are the next level down on the scale of obnoxiousness. They are not dangerous. They are more unsatisfying and dissatisfying as partners than they are lethal or brutal. For example, Gimmie Monie is after a man's money but she will not kill to get it; Psycho Babbler might stalk a man but she will not boil his pet rabbit and serve it for dinner. The cruel women and femme fatales of the movies take the Dirty Seven Sisters' selfishness into the realm of the illegal.

Why Do Crazy Girls Get away with It?

I'm all for girl power, so long as we aren't making men second class citizens. I just think that equality means that both sexes take responsibility for their bad behavior and poor manners as well as for their good actions. Most women aren't required to take responsibility for their sometime criminal actions. As in the case of my friend Holly, who called her ex Sonny about 200 times a day and followed him around 24/7.

If roles were reversed here, Sonny would have been arrested and charged, or at least served with a restraining order and I'm sure it would have made it into some local newspaper. But because Holly is female, we haven't learned of any legal actions taken. I'm sure it's because most men don't want to be laughed at by society and TONS of women use this to their advantage, to cause others pain. Isn't it amazing how my grandmother's burning of her bra has not made life any better for my daughter and me? It has just enabled abusive, strange, messed up women to get away with what they want, when they want it. Strange world....

❧

It does seem true that modern, post-industrial societies are more lenient toward abusive female behaviors. Women in other societies, who are kept under strict rules of behavior under penalty of being beaten or killed, do not get the chance to display their personalities as Dirty Seven Sisters. They do not have the time or the means to stalk or harass a man. However, the vast majority of incarcerated violent criminals in the United States are male (over 96%). While it is true that women seem to get away with more in the eyes of the law, in general the majority of women do not resort to violence to solve their problems.

Statistically, females account for only 15% of all violent crime. Very few female serial killers exist in proportion to the number of male serial killers. Most female serial killers poison their victims rather than shooting or stabbing them. Even though Carol Wuornos shot her victims, she did not torture them before killing them. No reports exist of a female who has consumed the flesh of her serial victims like Jeffrey Dahmer and others. Remember, the Dirty Seven Sisters are not criminals. They are selfish and a pain to live with, but they are not dangerous, except to a man's wallet or to his peace of mind and happiness.

Another Psycho-chick

My ex-girlfriend is twisted! She called my home even though it's been six years since we last dated. She told my wife that I was trying to track her down and she even had proof. Then she proceeded to play a tape of me to my wife, with whom I have three children, of a message I supposedly left her on her answering machine. It was my voice, but the tape must have been six years old. I love my wife and children and I would never risk losing them for anyone or anything. The girl even tracked down my family to find out my home number. She lied to them so she could call my wife.

When we go to New York on vacation she tries to find out where we will be staying to harass us. I can't even visit my old buddies because she hangs out with them in hopes that I will show up and she could get a glimpse of me. Before we broke up she showed me something that scared the hell out of me. It was a shrine of me. She had some of my pictures and clothes on an altar with candles. I was never so afraid of a chick in my life. But I figured I would move to Florida and wouldn't be bothered by her. Well, here I am six years later still dealing with it. She is still single and waiting for me. Help! I feel sorry for her next victim. Girl, get some help!

❧

It is dismaying that some women think that being in love with a man justifies hounding him, following him around, calling him at work and home, and disrupting his life. "But I love him," they will say, as if this justified the most heinous behavior. "I want him. I don't care that he is with someone else now. I will destroy that and have him all to myself. That witch he is with doesn't deserve him. When I get him away from her, I will show him how much I love him. How could he refuse such a love? Everyone would like to be loved the way I love him! The fact that I am willing to spend my whole day following him around should show him how much I love him!"

This kind of thinking shows a Dirty Seven Sister's typical selfishness. She does not see the impact of her harassment on the man she supposedly loves. She does not see how repugnant her clingy desperation makes her seem. He shudders to think of spending an hour with her, no less the rest of his life. She wants her own way, like a child in a toy store who thinks that a tantrum will force her parents into getting her what she wants. It only makes her more unappealing and borders on the criminal.

Men, be warned, if a woman acts this way before she moves in with you, she will invade your life further once she is ensconced in it. Snooping around your cell phone for numbers and examining your pockets will be a regular occurrence. Get used to the game of "Twenty Questions" every time you go out alone, that is, if you can get away from her long enough to be alone.

Am I Psycho?
I was seeing this man for two and a half months, not long at all, but I did start to like him a lot! I never fall for men, and I do mean never. It's really hard for me to get attached to someone, mainly because I'm really picky and find things wrong with the person. Anyway, so this was a big deal that I actually was really into this man! So into him that I lost my virginity to him! Big mistake. About a month after we "did it" he just stopped calling me and avoided my calls or any type of contact with me. I thought of the possibility that I was just a hit and run but I don't think that was it at all. He really did like me when we were together and I know he did. He'd call and always want to see me, even though he lived pretty far. We were getting along very well.

After he ended things (by being a pussy instead of just being straightforward with me), I called him more times than I should have--about five times a day for two to three weeks.

I also went to a club where I knew he would be. He claimed he didn't see me when I confronted him about not saying "Hi" to me. I then threw my mug of beer in his face.

I also did some crazy things that he found out about, like I stabbed a teddy bear he had given to me, and maybe did a few crank calls. I know it sounds so immature but I was so heart-broken. I couldn't believe that a man could do this, and to me, of all people! It's seven months later, and I'm nowhere near over him. I still miss the good times we shared and hope that one day we could be together. It is his birthday today, so I sit here thinking about him more than ever. He has a girlfriend now and seems to really care about her, but I can't move on! I've called his girlfriend and told her that I slept with him last Monday, even though it wasn't so.

I know that seven months is way too long to keep obsessing over this man! I never thought it would take this long to get over him. After three months I thought, "Wow this is it! I'm over him, finally!" But then weeks would go by and I'd find myself back to square one. I am now seeing some one else, whom I've known for almost two years. I know it's wrong to be with someone while thinking of someone else, but I thought that he could be the one to help me get over my obsession.

I was more wrong than ever! I find myself closing my eyes when I'm with him and praying that when I open them I'll be with the man I really want. I want to move away. As sad as it sounds, I think that's the only thing I can do to really help me get over it. I don't even think I need a second chance with the man I like. What I want is closure. He hates me and I don't want him to (because I called him a few times at four in the morning and also keyed his girlfriend's new car). Even though I should hate him, I can't. I just want him to at least talk to me, so we can be friends, or at least be able to say "Hi" to one another when we see each other. I'll admit I have my insecurities, but I'm not one of those girls who think, "Omigod, I'm so ugly, and fat" and this and that. I know I'm really good looking and thin for the most part, but that always has me wondering, "What could his current girlfriend have, that I don't?" I know he's not using her because he calls her "my girlfriend." He never admitted that I was. They've been together now for like, four months and they still haven't had sex! How do I know this? Maybe I am a little psycho and have done my share of investigating. Do you think I am a psycho?

Yes, I think you are acting like a standard psycho. Obsessing over your brief relationship with this man will not make him change his mind and come back to you. Trying to force attraction and attachment does not work and actually backfires.

I understand that getting dumped can bruise even the most confident ego. But we all experience getting dumped at least once in our lives. Understand this, reconcile yourself with it, mend your ego, and move on with your life. This is not easy for obsessive people. Some spend years in counseling attempting to overcome it. When people are obsessed, they think about the other person at least 80% of their waking hours and also dream about them at night. Yet no one person is worth devoting that much energy to, let alone mutilating a perfectly innocent teddy bear over.

Cyber-psycho

I am a man who happened to be on the receiving end of a psycho-chick's attentions. I only dated mine for a week. Yep, that's right, ONE WEEK!

She left me I don't know how many crazy messages. She even cut herself up when I told her it was over...AFTER A WEEK!

She also managed to cyberstalk me and send Instant Messages to my friends. She threatened suicide, she tried the guilt trips, she threatened my health, and on and on.

I'm not a young man, I'm almost 30, and she's in her 30's. You wouldn't expect that kind of psycho crap from a woman that old.

I honestly believed she'd hunt me down and kill me. Thank God I never showed her where I live and thank God for the fact that she was afraid to leave her house.

The problem was that I didn't know what I was getting into. She seemed normal to start with, and when I started noticing signs of her nuttiness I was willing to try to see past it. By the first date she was already talking about marriage and having babies. On the second date she was falling all over herself and acting like a complete fool, madly in love with me and our future together.

So I slowed things down a bit, and eventually told her that we should just be friends. I tried to let her down easy, and I'm a nice man, so I told her that we could still talk because she definitely needed someone to talk to sometimes. BIG MISTAKE!

She went completely nuts. She cut herself up with a knife, and even called me while she was doing it. She talked about killing herself and I honestly thought she'd do it. I should have called the cops. I should have sent them over to her place to get her. But she threatened to kill me if I did. What was I supposed to do? This went on way into the early morning. I didn't want to hang up and have the weight of someone's suicide on my shoulders. So I went over there.

Again, BIG MISTAKE! I had no bad intentions in going over there. I just wanted to try to be her friend and make sure she made it through the night. Then, even through my best efforts to combat it, we ended up having sex. If I had to do it over I wouldn't have done it.

I had to tell her again that we're just friends. No funny stuff anymore! But she wasn't having it. She called several times alternating between downright abusive behavior and sobbing apologies. She'd love me one minute, hate me the next, threaten me, and then apologize. I gave up on the taking-it-easy tactic and went for the harsh approach.

I finally stopped talking to her, didn't take her calls, figured she'd take the hint. But she didn't. My voicemail filled up every day with drama upon drama, accusations, tears, threats, and pleading. The messages to my friends too were embarrassing and ridiculous. I laugh about it, but it was definitely not normal behavior. It's strange listening to the voicemails here now.

The really scary part? I was only seeing her for a week, a measly week!

❧

You were doing all right until your confession of sleeping with this girl, right after you had spent the entire night trying to keep her from killing herself over the loss of you in her life. It is just plain stupid that you slept with her after all your misgivings about her. Going all the way over to her place to sleep with her, makes you look even more unwise.

You knew she was moving way too fast, in typical Needee Nellie fashion, talking about marriage on the first date and ready to kill herself when you broke up with her after one week of dating.

You went over there and had sex with her anyway. You are not responsible for her actions but you are most definitely responsible for yours. Taking advantage of a Needee Nellie is one of the easiest activities a man can undertake. Your story attempts to make her look bad but you are digging your own grave in the process!

You mention your ages and that you are not kids. There is no age limit on the Dirty Seven Sisters. They can be just as impossible to be with at 20 as they are at 30, 40, 50 and beyond. That is one of the distinguishing characteristics of the Dirty Seven Sisters: They do not improve over time and sometimes get worse.

Why Do I Keep Attracting PMS Queens?

I went with this girl for a year. We also lived together. About four months into the relationship, she started telling me about how her period made her act crazy. But she didn't need to tell me that. I saw it for myself, except that usually a woman's period lasts for about five days and her PMS behavior lasted 24/7/365.

She got really crazy on me! When we would get into an argument she would scream at the top of her lungs, slam doors, throw things, her face red, her eyes bulging. She would then pace back and forth like a caged panther. I wanted to leave my own house to get away for awhile after the fight and she would start crying saying, "You can't leave! I might hurt myself!"

There were times when I got home late from work and she called my cell phone twenty times, wondering why I was ten minutes late. She called my family too! Crazy! She went through my stuff to see if I was cheating on her. She asked me if she should exercise because she thought she was fat. I told her to do what she wanted. Then she flipped out on me saying that I don't love her and that she is fat and ugly! Things progressively got worse as time went on.

We finally broke up after she came to my job and had a screaming fit right in front of my boss. That was the final straw. I told her she was too much like my last girlfriend, who pulled some of the same insane stunts. She still calls me almost every week, at home and at work, saying, "I love you," then the next day saying, "I hate you!" This has been going on for five months. If I don't answer the phone she will come to my house to see why! I told her last night to stop calling me, for good! I don't know how many times that came out of my mouth with my last girlfriend too! Why does this keep happening to me? It took me three years to get rid of my last girlfriend and now it is happening again!

க

People are doomed to keep repeating the same relationship patterns, until they recognize their specific ruts and thus begin to break out of them. The fact that you selected this book shows you are on your way to understanding the PMS Queen's pattern and to recognizing that they make her a failure in maintaining happy relationships. If you keep attracting that kind of female companionship, you may not feel you are worthy of anything better. You may move too quickly and allow her into your life too soon, due to your own needs.

Now that you have seen that your girlfriends fit a certain pattern, take the time and thought to break out of your own mistaken choices. You may have become addicted to the drama and think that non-moodswingers are boring. If this is true, you will continue to choose the histrionic hissy-fitters of the world. But if you really want to break the pattern, do not enter hastily into your next relationship. Especially, do not move in together until you see how the woman behaves under all sorts of conditions, not just on a date. On the typical date, particularly in the early stages, even the PMS Queen can keep her disorderly mindset hidden with small talk and flirtations. But because she lacks self-control, her pretenses will fray, exposing the ragged edges of her true personality as time goes on.

Men are from Hell, Women are from Purgatory
I'm tired of all the books proposing that we all understand each other better. What's to understand? Either the woman or man behaves like a decent human being or they don't. If they don't, then have the self-respect to get away from them. I think it's a waste of time to try to understand why a person misbehaves, as if spending years on a psychiatrist's couch is going to somehow make them easier to live with. If a person is a shallow gold-digger, understanding why she is that way doesn't make her all of a sudden deep and thoughtful or a relationship with her happy.

This is true. That is why the position of this book is purely behavioral. Actions, not words and intentions, are what matter. A person may be a Needee Nellie or a Shopaholica because of deep insecurities stemming from childhood abandonment. Regardless of the cause, the Shopaholica is incapable of committing her heart to one man because somebody better might come along at any minute. Needee Nellie will still cling to you like crazy glue and make an annoyance of herself.

Genetic Determinism
Aren't we predisposed to pick our mates based on our gene's selectivity? Physical beauty equals genetic health

and is attractive to a male who is driven to propagate the species through sexual activity. Furthermore, our genes trigger and receive unseen signals, such as pheromones, that clinch the mating experience. Scientists have postulated that even our immune systems (certain variable immune proteins) play a role in our choice of a mate. If our genes are making the decisions for us, how can we avoid the traps of the Dirty Seven Sisters? If one of these disastrous mates sends out the right genetic signals, a man can be swept into the mating vortex regardless of the woman's behavior. She can then be like the black widow spider or praying mantis, programmed to kill and eat their mates as part of the coupling experience.

ॐ

This is why I state at the beginning of this book that we must override our continuous thrust to mate, driven by the emotional brain and unconscious mind. Instead, we must use our rational minds and set behavioral standards. If we do not, our relationships will crash and burn after many hours of misery and incompatibility. Moreover, the poor mothering qualities of our mates will have harmful effects on our children in the future and will not be of benefit to the happy survival of the species as a whole. The psycho-babbling, emotionally overwrought mother will replicate herself in her offspring unless there is total rebellion against her as the child's role model. The mindless materialism of The Material Girl will produce grabby little kids devoid of heart and feelings (except excitement over acquisition and the drive for more--unless they too rebel and decide to base their lives on other values).

Combo Sisters

It seems so cut and dried that all rotten women fall into seven neat categories. Couldn't a woman be a combination of several of the Dirty Seven Sisters?

کہ

You are correct in assuming that combinations of the Dirty Seven Sister types exist. In proportion to the number of types blended in one woman, the more difficult it is to live on a daily basis with her. For example, a Needee Nellie combined with a PMS Queen combined with a Psycho Babbler makes for a particularly whiny, shrewish mate who wants to talk about her misery at all times. The Wedding Belle combined with The Mom makes for a boring companion who wants to trap and boss you for the rest of your days. Some women combine all of the types in a variety of ways: A money-grubbing, appearance obsessed, screaming psycho who belittles you in public yet follows you around night and day, might be an example of Gimmie Monie combined with Prettie Pennie, the Psycho Babbler, The Mom, and Needee Nellie.

COUNTERPARTS OF

THE DIRTY SEVEN GUYS

Female Counterparts

In my previous book, *The Dirty Seven: Ladies Beware!*, I describe seven types of males that are not mate-material. They are looking for a relationship but they are not up to the task because of excessive me-ism or the ability to feel empathy for someone else. I also describe the female counterparts to the Dirty Seven guys. These female counterparts are slightly different from the more disturbing Dirty Seven Sisters found in this book. They fall more into the annoying and dismaying category, rather than the life-destroying species described within these pages. These female counterparts of the Dirty Seven guys are:

- **ScarBaby:** She goes on and on about her ex and everyone else who ever dumped her. Her date is her shrink. She is bitter and cynical.

- **SideCar:** She has her little flings on the side and lies about them, but makes no promises. She is sometimes looking for the love she is missing in her main relationship or validation as a beautiful woman because she has already become part of the furniture to her husband or boyfriend.

- **CrazyWoman:** Her behavior is bizarre and ritualistic. She may believe she is a witch and has altars in every room of the house. She might dance as she drums on a tom-tom drum while howling at the moon.

- **LadyLady:** Prefers members of her own gender to those of the opposite sex, and hides it instead of letting you know up front. Her preference emerges later when she runs off with another woman.

- **GIRLie:** (Gee, I'm Really Lost) is Little Girl Lost and does not take good care of herself and definitely cannot care for others. She is the scared rabbit who appeals to the Rescuer. Help me, help me, is her message.

- **OLLady:** Even when she gets up in years, she still acts like "Helpless Little Me." Her expectations for getting taken care of diminish, however. As her looks fade, her Poor Little Me routine loses whatever cuteness it may have had in the distant past.

- **BagLady:** She has lots of kids, pets, relatives that meddle, and a few exes. Her life is a whirlwind of activities caring for others. She may become dependent on the guy to help her manage all of this, especially financially, and it is way more than he bargained for.

Epilogue

I am not a psychotherapist or a psychoanalyst, so some may ask, "What gives her the right to record her observations about female behavior on the dating and mating front?" As a writer, high school teacher, corporate trainer, seminar speaker, and fitness instructor, I have learned in the living laboratory of human interaction. I have dealt with human beings in social and work settings rather than with laboratory rats in cages.

The material I discuss herein cannot be found in the pages of the psychoanalytical textbooks. These books focus on causes of behaviors. A few focus on behavioral modification. But none focus on the strange phenomena of modern dating patterns and traps. Freud explains that we have certain fixations resulting from unmet needs in childhood. Thus a man might seek out The Mom to compensate for his original lack. If this is so, a shrewish, bossy spouse may be his key to happiness and this book is of no worth to him.

Because I am not a psychiatrist, I do not talk about the causes for the poor behaviors of the Dirty Seven Sisters. I do not go into why some men are masochistic enough to stay in unloving, unhappy relationships with them. I am only addressing the man who has his head together, is not living out some deep-seated neurosis, and is seeking a female companion he can be with, joyfully, freely, and gratefully.

I come from the behaviorists' point of view: Who cares why

these people are the way they are? The fact is, they behave this way. It is their behavior that I am dealing with now, not the childhood trauma, or whatever, that may have caused it. They can be any way they want away from me, but if they cannot behave within certain boundaries in my presence on a consistent basis, I don't need them intimately involved in my life. I wish them well as I send them on their way. Their confrontational, clingy, shallow, obsessed, bossy, and difficult behaviors are relationship killers.

Both the Dirty Seven and the Dirty Seven Sisters are difficult to live with on a daily basis. In the case of the guys, it is their total oblivion to their partners' point of view that makes them me-centered disasters as mates. In the case of the sisters, it is not as easy to pigeonhole, except that these women are the cause of extreme disappointment if you are looking for love, delight, and comfort. Their bait and switch tactics, the one thing most of them have in common, hide their characteristic behaviors until it is too late. You, like so many other unfortunate guys, could end up booby trapped by them. My aim in writing this book was to make sure you don't, by giving you the tools to find true love and happiness.

ABOUT THE AUTHOR

June Marshall, author of *Booby Trapped: Men Beware! The Dirty Seven Sisters* and *The Dirty Seven: Ladies Beware!* was born in Sao Paolo, Brazil to American parents. They moved back to the United States while she was a child. After finishing college, she went to New York to study acting and singing, along with earning a Masters in English Literature. She then moved to Europe, where she lived in Belgium and visited the major cities of the continent. Next came her "Passage to India," where she traveled from its southernmost tip to the Himalayas. Her familiarity with diverse cultures of the world originates from these experiences and flavors her unique philosophy. It has also greatly contributed to her understanding of human nature.

Her career, so far, has included being a Writer, Public Speaker and Speech Writer, English Teacher, Actor-Singer, and even being Webmaster and Systems Usability Engineer at AT&T.

She has appeared on television and radio as well as given talks and seminars on the topic of mateability, behavioral standards, and selectivity in the dating arena. She has also written numerous articles for various publications.

Her concepts for her first two books took shape in 1981 when she was newly single in New York City, after a divorce. She noticed that certain types of men (The Dirty Seven) and women (the Dirty Seven Sisters) were actively seeking life partners and yet they were not behaviorally or emotionally equipped to sustain such relationships. She observed the havoc wrought in her friends' and acquaintances' lives by these unsuitable mates. Twenty years later, she was again single and out in the dating marketplace. Once again these types asserted themselves. The idea had stood the test of time. The Dirty Sevens are still out there, actively seeking mates. They are still as unsuitable for consumption as certain types of poisonous mushrooms, which may look tempting but are deadly.

Not one to sit on her laurels for long, she is already at work on her next-to-be published book, *The Second Marshall Plan: Making the World Safe for Love and Happiness*. It will present her approach to some of human life's deepest issues: The search for meaning, the need for love, and social structures that impede what they purport to achieve.

June has two grown daughters and lives in the New York metropolitan area.

This book and its companions are, or will also be, available in one or more of the following editions:

- Audio book tape
- Audio book CD
- Ebook
- Video tape

Please visit our web site, listed on the next page, as often as you wish to find out when they become available. Or sign up for our quarterly newsletter *Links to Me*dia*, to keep abreast of our releases.

CREDITS, COPYRIGHTS, AND LINKS

Author:	June Marshall
Editor & designer:	Steven Kingsley

COPYRIGHTS

Story:	©June Marshall 2003. All rights reserved.
Cover design:	NewMedia Publishing 2003
Cover image:	Computer generated with the following open source (Linux) software: Blender 2.26 3D Modeler from blender.org GIMP 1.2.2 from gimp.org
Celebrity stories:	Compiled from 2001, 2002, and 2003 print, radio, TV, cable, and online editions of: AClassCelebs.com Ananova.com BBC News CNN.com Counterpunch.org Entertainment Weekly eOnline Celeb Courthouse National Enquirer SingingDivas.com Sunday Times South Africa SwinginChicks.com TheSmokingGun.com WENN Radio

LINKS

Publisher:	www.newmediapublishing.com

CPSIA information can be obtained at www.ICGtesting.com
Printed in the USA
LVOW06s2138070813

346878LV00002B/85/A